Ideas in History

Journal of the Nordic Society
for the History of Ideas

Volume 9, no. 1–2

2015

Museum Tusculanum Press
University of Copenhagen

Ideas in History
Journal of the Nordic Society for the History of Ideas
© 2015 Museum Tusculanum Press, Copenhagen
Cover design: Erling Lynder
ISBN 978 87 635 4396 5
ISSN 1890 1832

About the Journal
Ideas in History has been the result of collaborative efforts among nearly a dozen universities and colleges throughout the Nordic countries. The purpose of these initiatives has been to further awareness of research, resources and activities in the field of intellectual history in the Nordic countries as well as internationally. The journal has aimed to create a meeting ground for the study of ideas in historical context across disciplinary, geographical and institutional boundaries. *Ideas in History* has welcomed interdisciplinary approaches to intellectual history at the same time that it has acknowledged specific traditions in the field. *Ideas in History* has sought a pluralism of methodological approaches to intellectual history: reflections on the field, historical contexts studied, subject matter for intellectual-historical investigation, critical understandings of relations between the intellectual past and present as well as the comprehension of culturally, politically and geographically diverse intellectual traditions.

Acknowledgements
Ideas in History is published with the financial assistance of the Nordic Board for Periodicals in the Humanities in the Humanities and Social Sciences. Ideas in History also wishes to thank the Department of Philosophy, Classics, History of Art and Ideas at the University of Oslo for its previous support support of the editorial administration of this journal.

Manuscripts
This is *Ideas in History*'s final issue. The journal will therefore no longer be accepting submissions.

Subscription
Museum Tusculanum Press
University of Copenhagen
Birketinget 6
DK-2300 Copenhagen S, Denmark
Tel. +45 32 34 14 14 / Fax +45 32 58 14 88
Email order@mtp.dk / www.mtp.dk

Contents

Intellectual Historiographies of Human Rights: Comment and Meaning

Ben Dorfman[1]

Abstract

Taking the form of a book review and interpretive essay, this article looks at intellectual-historical debates concerning the origins of rights and contextualizes them against problems of rights politics. Three relatively recent texts, Samuel Moyn's *The Last Utopia: Human Rights in History* (2010), Lynn Hunt's *Inventing Human Rights: A History* (2007) and Paul Gordon Lauren's *The Evolution of International Human Rights: Visions Seen* (1998) have problematized the dating of rights and the proximity of rights ideas to our own times. On their own, these are interesting intellectual-historical problems – from whence do some of our most cherished ideals come? Such questions are also, however, the bases for senses of the absoluteness and globality of rights, or lack thereof, and the particular politics societies make around rights applicability and conceptualization. This positions a particular part of rights debates – intellectual-historical debates – closer to the heart of rights politics than we normally think.

It may be cliché to say that human rights are the "pressing issue of our times" – the narrative of rights often depending on a particular kind of drama (see Slaughter 2007). There might be some truth to the idea, though. Whether it is bombing Syria – ISIS, anyway – commenting on the topsy-turvy nature of Egyptian politics since the start of 2011's "Arab Spring" or discussing the meaning of China's increasing emergence as a world power, rights have significant play on the world agenda (e.g., Ellis 2014; DW 2015; Myers and Schmitt 2013). You can't "avoid" rights, historian Kenneth Cmiel (2004, 117) has argued, and it's a good point. Here, Cmiel points to rights as norm as much as incontrovertible sets of truths and ethical senses we might invoke regardless of time or place. It's an observation about the dominance of rights a number of scholars have made.[2]

---

1 Ben Dorfman is associate professor of intellectual and cultural history in the Department of Culture and Global Studies at Aalborg University.

2 See also Andreopoulos and Arat (2014); Douzinas (2000); Bobbio (1996).

Intellectual history has a particular role in rights. It's an interesting phenomenon: among rights scholars, though they often *do* brands of intellectual history (e.g., Donnelly 2003; Beitz 2009; Weissbrodt and de la Vega 2007), it's little-thematized as such. Often, it's but given that one might date human rights to 1648 and the Peace of Westphalia, 1945 and the foundation of the United Nations or perhaps the 1790s and the publication of Kant's "Towards Perpetual Peace" (1795) (Woods 2014). Other concepts show up too: Roman law notions of *ius gentium* and *ius naturale*, revolutionary declarations from France and America at the end of the eighteenth century and Stoic, Aristotelian and Platonic branches of Greco-Roman philosophy have all been invoked as setting the table for rights thought (see Ishay 2004). In many ways, this is correct. Using a weak definition of intellectual history as a notion "attending [temporally] ... to concepts" (Kelley 1990, 20) (I intentionally stay away from debates about what "concepts" are), it's clear that modes of historical investigation having a particular wax and wane over the past number of years ("intellectual history") are central to rights (on the history of intellectual history, see Kelley 2002). The Canadian lawyer John Humphrey (in Normand and Zaidi 2008, 147) once offered that "defin[ing] and regulat[ing] the relationship between the individual and Society" is an essential part of rights. Rights involving speculation on broad swaths of concepts and events impacting significant segments of societies we call our own. This includes senses of justice, international law and the meaning of ethical standards used to create the moralities present on the multiple levels of social experience on which all of us exist. Intellectual history is part of this project.

Over the past ten years or so, two books with an intellectual-historical bent addressing human rights have garnered a relatively high degree of attention: Samuel Moyn's *The Last Utopia: Human Rights in History* (2010) and Lynn Hunt's *Inventing Human Rights: A History* (2007). In these well-received works, both authors deconstruct the history of human rights from what Moyn (2010, 8) terms its "church" form. By "church form" is meant rights as age-old ideas towards which humanity has necessarily been marching all along – a kind of *Ur*-concept towards which humanity marches as it "matures." For academics, challenging such arguments might be second nature. Teleological history was thrown out with the bathwater of utopian politics years ago and "counter-memory," as a more Foucauldian vocabulary (1977) would have it, is much more in vogue. Still, rights scholarship, to say nothing rights activism, occupies an interesting spot – deconstructing ideas one might analytically know are "built," yet sometimes wanting to pose them as natural anyway because, for many of us, fundamental rights define significant parts of worlds we want. The line between scholar and activist can be thin, and the remnants of tele-ological history not easy to disband.[3]

Theses like Moyn's and Hunt's pose themselves against works like Micheline R. Ishay's *The History of Human Rights: From Ancient Times to the Globalization Era* (2004) and perhaps especially, Paul Gordon Lauren's *The Evolution of International Human Rights: Visions Seen* (1998). Indeed, Lauren's book has in particular been advanced as the "standard" history of rights – an account of rights more or less in tack with what the United Nations or organizations like Amnesty or Human Rights Watch would like to promote (Afshari 2007). Roughly (see Dorfman 2014; Slaughter 2007), this involves senses that though rights have been a struggle and history is marked by their loss as much as gain, there's still a broad sense in which all humanity might recognize rights concerns – a human recognition demonstrating rights as inexorable ethical impulses emerging from all of us under the right circumstances and at the right time. This idea suggests that temporally and historically, rights show up anytime religions say "thou shalt" (or "thou shalt not") or one brings morality into the constitution of the regional, national or international politics. Using Rousseau's (1969, 49) vocabulary, it's the sense that, remove the "chains" and rights, if not "freedom," in the human sphere will shine through.

My goals here are modest. Largely, I'm interested to look at the interpre-tations of rights offered by Moyn, Hunt and Lauren and think about their meanings. Specifically, I'd like to stick my toe in the waters of those involved in debates about how *old* rights are – *human* rights – and see what they say. In a way, that's important in itself. Debates about the "origins" of human rights occupy the background of the field (see Perry 2000; Bietz 2009; Donnelly 2003), and there's always a sense, regardless of the topic, in which one needs to lay out legacies and origins. Books like Moyn's, Hunt's and Lauren's are precisely about such problems. However, I'd also like to think about the *con-sequences* of such debates. I.e., through the course of the twentieth century, though perhaps especially over the past twenty or thirty years, rights' popular-ity has grown. The "age of rights," as Norberto Bobbio (1996) put it, involves debates over whose rights apply where, when and why – debates asking into rights history, where the concept was developed and how. I'm not particularly concerned with "how." The departure into causality involves an entry into his-

3 There can be a "moralist-political instrumentalization" of rights scholarship, it has been suggested, where activism and academics are difficult to dissect. It's not always easy to be a rights scholar without being a rights promoter. See Kammerhoffer (2012).

toriographical intricacies too great for this article to bear. Still, even framed
in terms of "when" and "where" – signposts, as such, concerning where rights
come from – the intellectual history of rights carries broad meaning in terms
of thinking through rights policy and the components of claims actors make
concerning the relevance of rights ideas to our times and world. Very simply,
I'd like to take that apart a bit, and see what it means for rights politics and
their application. To non-intellectual historians, "history of ideas" – some
sort of tracing of concepts – might appear a bit dusty. Randall Jarrell (1954)
once portrayed the well-heeled as keeping a copy of the *Journal of the History
of Ideas* next to *Town and Country* on their coffee tables as a measure of urban-
ity. Those days are gone. Potentially, however, the field gains an extra shot of
juice when attached to the relevance of an idea many of us seem to hold dear
and around which a great number of contemporary debates seem to unfold.
It's time we recognize that, when one discusses human rights, one is always
playing, to some extent, the game of intellectual history.

Samuel Moyn: Über-Skeptic

I start with Moyn – and call him the "über-skeptic" – because few have engen-
dered more *doubting* the standard history of rights than he. Reviewing *The
Last Utopia* for *Human Rights Quarterly* Adam Etinson (2012, 295) has summa-
rized the "standard" history as follows:

> After a lengthy post-Enlightenment slumber [via which the Enlighten-
> ment birthed rights], human rights recaptured the global imagination
> in the aftermath of the Second World War and, in particular, the Holo-
> caust….[P]ostwar revulsion to Nazi brutality culminated in the interna-
> tional signing of the 1948 Universal Declaration of Human Rights. Since
> then…we've witnessed is gradual dissemination of the moral wisdom
> embodied in that document… [That has come] in the form of a growing
> affirmation of human rights across the globe, and in the form of the pro-
> gressive introduction of human rights into domestic and international
> law.

Etinson captures the situation nicely. Positive senses of rights abound, and
they often go unthought. I'd suggest, however, Etinson, may *downplay* certain
dimensions of the "standard history." First, as Bryan Turner (2011, 678) notes
in *his* review of Moyn's work, rights historians are often persuaded to look at
specific historical events such as the French Revolution or American War of

Independence as the roots of human rights thought. Here, a range of Enlightenment and proto-Romantic thinkers from Locke to Kant to Rousseau enter the picture – wherein rights don't just emerge from a "post-Enlightenment slumber," but rather come from a specific set of tendencies *in* Enlightenment thought. It's an increasingly popular idea. In his attempt to resurrect something of a Peter Gay-esque progressive Enlightenment, for example, Jonathan Israel (2011, 12) directly attaches the major streams in seventeenth- and eighteenth-century European and North American philosophy to a "package" of "basic human rights" – the idea of an amelioratory social politics and positive political change. "Equality, democracy and freedom" Israel (2010, 12) suggests, were the hallmarks of Enlightenment idealism. Kantian ideas (2006a) that all might emerge from their self-imposed "immaturity" and have the courage to use one's own understanding were ideas not present in the *ancien* régime. That didn't make "Atlantic" revolutions popular revolutions (Palmer 2014). It doesn't transform the Enlightenment into an age of popular awakening. It makes the Enlightenment "radical," though (Israel 2001), and a movement seeking rational grounds for politics that would accept no truck and little opposition.

It's also the case that the Enlightenment in itself isn't always the limit for tracing rights. Turner (2011, 678), e.g., notes that some – David Aune (2013) and Ishay (2004) are examples – posit rights cosmopolitanism and universalism as going back to the Stoics, or perhaps Paul's letters to the Galatians or notions of rationality and "the good life" embedded in the roots of Greco-democratic thought. Again, complexities abound. We'll also get into "ancient" ideas of rights with Lauren. However, some scholars (e.g., Dorfman 2014) note this makes rough play on concepts presented by human rights *themselves.* We're "born" with rights, the documents like Universal Declaration (United Nations 1948, article 1) note – the Universal Declaration standing as foundational international rights document – and, despite histories of "barbarism," there's no way to doubt liberty's inherent nature given the capacities for "reason and conscience" with which all human beings born. Again, we'll circle around to these kinds of arguments with Lauren. However, it's noteworthy that *rights* – rights themselves – posit their origins with the birth of humanity itself. Surely, 1776, 1789, 1848 or any other "typical" rights date was important to human rights progenitors. Figures like René Cassin explicitly pointed to the French Revolution as inspiration (see Ishay 2004, 3). Still, the UN would have us believe, if you put your ear closely enough to the rails, you can hear the locomotive of human rights chugging down the track as easily in ancient times as modern, and in non-Western locales as much as the Western geographies in which we often imagine rights to have gotten their start. It's a history they'd like us to adopt, and of which they most certainly want us to all be aware.

Moyn won't have any of this. Generally, he makes two moves to break these kinds of concepts. Firstly, he remakes 1948. Typically, Moyn suggests, 1948 is taken as something of an international 1789. Principles of inherent right previously viewed in *national* contexts were *inter*nationalized as the notion of the intrinsic worth of human beings was put in truly intrinsic terms (i.e., the inherentness of rights was extended across all regio-national borders and made fully universal [a "rights revolution," Michael Ignatieff (2000) has called it]). In a way, Moyn assents to this idea. *Previous* to 1948, he suggests (Moyn 2010, 26), rights involved a "whole people incorporating itself in a state." *Before* the UN and Universal Declaration – dates like 1776, 1789, or 1848 – the issue was creating *citizenries* that might enjoy inherent rights as opposed to formulations of *international* communities where all were "citizens" regardless of whether they belonged to a state or not (a marked problem in human rights [see Weissbrodt 2008]). Very simply, we can't ignore the nationalist dimensions of eighteenth- and nineteenth-century Europe. In another way, however, that was exactly the point. What marked *human* rights as opposed to earlier iterations of rights (the French *droits de l'homme*, e.g.) was that by and large eighteenth-century rights were *but* national. The French declared democracy for the French; the Americans for Americans. In 1848, broader European revolutions sought *national* sovereignty over and above an "internationalism" that might be theoretically present. Even the most internationalist thinkers – Kant would be an example – posed the international community as build up off of national communities, and national sovereignty as the primary issue with which rights should be concerned.[4] The notion of human rights as extending back to the Enlightenment, to say nothing of earlier, becomes exaggerated. For Moyn (2010, 28), that's because no one had in mind the "full bodied" protection of rights for *all* individuals regardless of citizenship *until* the 1940s. In essence, one doesn't get human rights in any concrete sense until the UN proclaimed them, and then did so again more systematically

---

4 Moyn (2010, 28) denotes Kant as a potential exception. In fact, Kant (2006b, 73, 70) discussed "cosmopolitan right" – a notion of a "universal state of humankind." Still, Kant also argues strongly for the sovereignty of states: "no state shall forcibly interfere in the constitution or government of another state." Moreover, the international community was formed of citizens *of* states. For Moyn, this is the mark of an intellectual culture, even in in its most radical forms, unable to break away from the national ideal.

when it created the Universal Declaration in 1948 after a three-year delibera-
tion as to their precise shape and nature.

It's a provocative thesis. However, I'll put a pin in Moyn's "rights from the
1948" idea for a moment in part to highlight the *second* move Moyn makes
to disturb the traditional rights narrative – again, rights extending to the
Enlightenment or before. That's to suggest that the "breakthrough," as
another volume of his calls it (Moyn and Eckel 2013) – the moment at which
human rights *really* became a global issue – wasn't the 1940s, but the *1970s*.
Indeed, this is the point for which Moyn has received the most attention.
Now, concretely, it's hard to say if this is an intellectual-historical as much as
social-historical point. The question may be less when the rights *concept* was
born than when it gained traction in global discourse and became an article
of social use. Still, it's provocative. Moyn contends that often we look through
rose-colored lenses and turn *all* independence and liberation movements into
human rights movements. Anti-colonialism, American Civil Rights, Gandhi's
struggle for Indian independence, African and Southeast Asian decoloniza-
tion – all, Moyn suggests, have become pillars of movements for universal
rights. "Become," though, is the key word. The reality, Moyn suggests, is that
such movements often concerned nationhood. "Self-determination" (Moyn
2010, 117) was the primary issue, and the problem was, in the spirit of the
name, escaping empire as opposed to instituting a new international system.
Try though we might, it's hard to find the full international spirit in what
were largely movements in *national* contexts. The tactic is clear. Over and
above theses such as Lauren's, Moyn goes after high profile rights champions
such as Michael Ignatieff (2000; 2001) – champions promoting rights as a
slow-bubbling "moral revolution" (Moyn 2010, 6) over extended periods of
time. Again, rights "moral revolution" might extent to the Enlightenment.
Rights "moral revolution" might extend to antiquity and the dawn of Western
civilization. At the very least, however, Moyn suggests, we often suppose we
can be *sure* rights were increasingly on people's minds through the course
of the *twentieth* century. Yes, Moyn contends, one *heard* of rights. There were
smatterings of rights vocabularies in early NGOs and from figures like Orson
Welles and Pope Pius XI (Moyn 2010, 44–83). However, it was only *after* anti-
colonialism, anti-imperialism, anti-racism and gender liberation movements
had taken hold that they were *retrospectively* fitted with a full-blown vision of
human rights. In a telling passage, Moyn (2010, 90) notes Gandhi as responding with "puzzlement" when UNESCO consulted him about what he thought
about "human rights." Like many activists even in the 1940s, '50s and '60s,

international rights apparently hadn't much come to mind for the Mahatma. The concept simply wasn't present in the ways we're used to.

What *really* happened, Moyn contends, was dissatisfaction with the Cold War. Human rights (Moyn 2010, 133) became a "novel framework for a series of genuine movements" doubting both the Soviet and American systems. Much comes into the picture: 1968 and the "Prague Spring," Vietnam and anti-Apartheid protest, peace activism, anti-nukes and perhaps especially Soviet Bloc dissidents as a *cause célèbres* (Andrei Sakharov appears extensively in Moyn's book). It was a slow, multi-angle encroachment in which ranges of students, intellectuals and politicians took up the cases of counter-culture and dissidence and began to wonder at the virtue of Cold War belligerents. The notion of human rights became the one "pure" struggle in an otherwise impure world. Indeed, Moyn suggests, things became really interesting when rights seeped into the spaces of state power. Especially when the Americans comprehended the rhetorical power of human rights in variety of settings – criticizing the Soviets, undermining Cuba's role in the Americas and gaining unexpected leverage during the 1972–5 Helsinki Process (Moyn 2010, 143) – momentum built to where they couldn't be ignored. All of a sudden, Moyn notes, from gay rights to women's rights to the Helsinki Watch organizations (rights monitoring organizations the Helsinki Accords allowed in the East), everything was "human rights." It was dramatic and "unexpected," Moyn (2010, 8) contends. Indeed, "unexpected" is the key word as it denaturalizes any longer term attachment to rights ideals and poses the dysfunctionality of mid-twentieth-century geo-politics as the root of their popularity if not the concept. In essence, we get an image of rights in which almost by accident, the UN reframes rights out of their national contexts in the late 1940s. This moment of broad idealism gets lost as Cold War powers retreat to their camps and forget internationalism. It comes back from the grass roots in the '70s, then begining the slow boil that spills over into today.

These are deeply provocative ideas deserving consideration. For one, they *do* disturb the metanarrative of rights. Politics shouldn't be "hagiography," Moyn (2010, 6) notes, and he sticks closely to that principle. Attacking the notion that rights might be ancient or persistent or "always present," Moyn dares to make a frontal assault on intuitively-held ideas. Again, over and above large-scales histories like Lauren's, it's a direct challenge to the 1900s as a "rights century" (see again Ignatieff 2000) and it indicates a less than smooth expansion of rights concepts whether one sees that as a twentieth-century event or not. The notion that there's been a steady growth in the institutions and practice of rights from antiquity to the present, or from the seventeenth and eighteenth centuries to the present or even more ancient times to the present gets a thorough browbeating. The documentary evidence, Moyn says, simply isn't there.

There are points here to quibble with too. Offering *her* review of Moyn's work, Jean Quataert (2011a, 1029) notes Moyn's omission of women. It's true, she notes, that movements like American civil rights and anti-Apartheid movements often sought to fit themselves into national frameworks; it was, after all, citizen's rights they primarily sought. The women's movement, though, was less co-optable. *Qua* network, it often appealed to human rights before the 1970s "breakthrough" as a way of heightening its appeal and because discrimination was often cultural as much as legal (i.e., national legal change wasn't enough [see Quataert 2011b]). Though the UN is important as the moment at which rights become *human* rights, Quataert suggests that Moyn also marginalizes that institution, seeing it largely seeing as a pawn of self-interested, *Realpolitical* actors (Normand and Zaidi 2008 make a not dissimilar point). It's fair enough. Both the Soviets and Americans used the UN as a proxy battleground, and few see the behaviors of state actors at the UN as pure. Still, it's hard to ignore how much rights legislation made it through the General Assembly in the 1960s – the International Covenant on Civil and Political Rights (1966), the International Covenant on Economic, Social and Cultural Rights (1966) and the International Convention on the Elimination of All Forms of Racial Discrimination (1965) are but a portion of the examples one could invoke. All actors had to moreover deal with the reality that human rights were in the UN Charter (1945) and theoretically commit themselves to their principles. Regional organizations, from the Council of Europe to the Organization of American States to the organization of African Unity also took up the rights cause. There's a question as to whether these organizations would have advanced the concept were it not imagined to have at least some power, and organizations like the UN hadn't promoted it and kept the heat on under the water. It doesn't undo the power of the book. However, one can question whether or not Moyn's is the *only* way to read the unfolding of rights (or lack thereof) between 1948 and the "take-off" years a quarter of a century later. At least for some, the answer might be "not."

Still, I see two points. Firstly, as Quataert notes (2011a, 1028), Moyn "naturalizes the presumed Western origins of human rights" [sic.]. While Moyn poses neither the Enlightenment nor ancient natural law nor any other archaic origin as rights' "true" roots, rights nonetheless represent an internationalization of at least certain vocabularies of American, British, French and other "Western" political traditions. The "insurmountable borders" of Europe's and North America's emerging nations in the late eighteenth and nineteenth centuries, Moyn (2010, 27) argues, relied on "abstract" principles. These were, at the end of the day, the "inalienable" concepts of self-determination and self-preservation around which rights organize themselves. "Early" rights, at least in the revolutionary Atlantic region, had some idea of the "universal." Here, Moyn is caught in a snafu. Though he downplays them, he isn't able to totally write-off the resemblance of human rights to the vocabularies of documents like the French and American Declarations or their intellectual predecessors (e.g., philosophers like Rousseau or Locke). In a way, rights *are* Enlightenment artifacts. Again, it exceeds his own argument. However, in Moyn's case we have reading where Western intellectual dominance lays down so many normative parameters that anything outside of liberal European traditions can't be seriously considered. Quataert (2011a, 1028) points out that Moyn "never questions" the Westernness of rights. She's right. If the UN is the father of human rights thought, modern European liberalism is its grandfather.

Still, identifying the Enlightenment as human rights' grandfather leaves the UN and the 1940s or at least immediate post-War years as their "fathers." I.e., the internationalization of rights that comes with the United Nations and the Universal Declaration does become decisive for Moyn, and it becomes an entry concerning when human rights "begin." Moyn and others in his circle emphasize the 1970s for good reason. They want to drive home when human rights became popular. Again, good observation. It isn't until the '70s that one gets large-scale rights movements, and their frequent adoption into social activist vocabularies. *Conceptually*, however, there's no doubt Moyn poses the 1945–1948 period, when the UN composed the Universal Declaration, as the breaking point. That's as it was in the late 1940s that human rights became *human*, and the requirements of citizenship needn't be invoked to "enjoy" rights. It's a provocative idea. The idea is that the new internationalisms of the immediate post-Second World War period weren't particularly popular, and it would be a quarter of decade until they were, challenges. That the world faced a new concept after the Second World War, however, is central. As Moyn poses it, discussing human rights previous to 1945 is a strained effort, and one might have to wait until 1948 and the passage of the Universal Declaration anyway. That is because it was then that the rights concept gained life in a systematic sense and as an idea we might recognize if not at all, then at least in ways that today are automatic or at least intuitive to many, if not most.

Hunt: Between Here and Beyond

Moyn's and Hunt's theses bridge each other in two ways. One is the denaturalization of rights. I.e., while Hunt doesn't explicitly say that human rights *don't* have intellectual roots in pre-Enlightenment thought – e.g., early modern theorization of international law like sixteenth-century jurist's Francisco de Vitoria's, or age old concepts of *ius naturale* or republican and democratic concepts in ancient Greece and Rome – she's clear that rights rest on two ideas: "autonomy" and "empathy" (Hunt 2007, 29). I.e., where Moyn poses internationalization, Hunt poses another set of concepts a bit more philosophical in nature and less about the *application* of rights as their heart. It leads to a different conclusion about the "age" problem, or how "old" human rights are, and that's as old as the Enlightenment and age of democratic revolutions on which Moyn wants to cast doubt.

There's a few elements to this argument. First, autonomy, as Hunt defines it, is "self-possession;" the notion that there are clear demarcations between you and I (the "centered" subject would be another vocabulary [a clear consciousness attached to a clear body (Turpin 2011, 138)]). "Autonomy" concerns notions that we have senses of who we are. It's an idea, Hunt notes, with a slow build through early modern philosophy into the period of "high" Enlightenment in the early and mid-eighteenth century. Empathy concerns mutual identification: that self-possessed subjects would recognize each other as similar – at least in their self-possession (i.e., we're all self-possessed beings). It's an essential democratic tenet. Subjects might establish different opinions – liberal societies, political theorist John Rawls (1993, 3–4) writes, incorporate (or at least can), "opposing and irreconcilable religious, philosophical and moral doctrines." *That* subjects are subjects, though – fellow human beings – can't be contravened. Partially, that's as the basis of *respecting* multiple opinions – the "epistemological egalitarianism" of the social body (Rorty 1996) – relies on the universality of subjective perception that allows us to be egalitarian. Again, it's a notion she finds coming through the spaces of Montesquieu, the *philosophes*, Pufendorf, Locke and other early philosophers of natural law and the potential of the free human being.

Hunt (2007, 29) poses autonomy and empathy as "cultural practices." I.e., through their social transmission concepts such as autonomy and empathy have to "go on." They have to be activated, somehow, within "minds" (wherein Hunt's intellectual history becomes a bit more psychological than Moyn's). Socially-developed relations with foundational rights ideas need to be established. Again, though in non-specific ways, Hunt (2007, 29) charges that "over the long term of several centuries, individuals had begun to pull themselves from the webs of community and…[became] increasingly independent as agents both legally and psychologically." A less individualistic, more spiritualistic, chivalric and absolutist medieval world was disappearing. The "world we have lost," as historian Peter Laslett (1965) termed a premodern world, faded away. Breaks with tradition experienced a "spurt," however, in the late eighteenth century (Hunt 20007, 30). As most reviewers of her book have noted (Martin 2008; Lawrence 2010; de Bolla 2009), Hunt's most provocative arguments here concern the arts: literature, architecture and painting. Events like the American and French Revolutions and their attendant rights documents are undoubtedly important – they're the politics of rights and rights clearly have their crests over the surface of world events. This was undoubtedly driven by new theories of liberty and social contracts emerging from Enlightenment salons and philosophical debate. Such events were increasingly digestible, however, due to the rise of reading cultures around novels like Samuel Richardson's *Clarissa* (1748) and Jean-Jacques Rousseau's *La Nouvelle Héloïse* (1761) as well as changing traditions in visual arts such as late eighteenth-century portraiture (the works of Joshua Reynolds would be good example). Noting a rough truth, Hunt (2007, 58) argues that these inculcated appreciation of the "emotional intensity of the ordinary" and the "capacity of people like [ourselves] to create on [our] own a moral world." The structure of what today might be called proto-Romanticism asks us to sympathize with the individual suffering of others. Again, Hunt focuses much on literature. Portraiture also took up the baton, however, by presenting clear individuals where the driving question was *individual* relations with the viewer as well as what the individual might do or accomplish in the future (in addition to Reynolds, the work of Gainsborough also comes to mind). That was compounded by yet further practices. Everyday emphases on hygiene and focus on the private home and senses of private space. Once, Hunt (2007, 94) argues, it wasn't conceivable that the "pain" of an individual's body or psyche might belong solely to themselves. The oppression or suffering a person might experience played into "higher religious and political purposes" – largely oriented towards hierarchical communities like the Church or absolutist society. Cultural practices made notions of inherent individuality more automatic, however. Minds chewed on the essence of human rights. To this extent, when Voltaire took up the case of Jean Calas's 1762 public torture (Calas was tortured for being a Protestant in Catholic France), he got a public ear. Calas was subject with rights. That was just like the rest of us.

This provides a second point two where Moyn and Hunt abut. I'm less versed in eighteenth century-cultural history than twentieth. However, at the ideological level, Hunt's claim is roughly that the vocabularies of "inherentness," or "inalienability" – used in both documents like the French and American Declarations as well as the Universal Declaration – and the notion of "abstract universalism" (Hunt 2007, 153) promoted in a spectrum of revolutionary philosophies and vocabularies are the basis of rights. Again, though Hunt invokes a cognitive-intellectual dimension – one can't imagine rights if one doesn't have the conceptual apparatuses to do so (hence the interest in art, literature and public torture) – this offers a surprising resonance with Moyn. *Prima facie*, Hunt doesn't reject the idea that the era of the mid-eighteenth century to the mid-nineteenth was in the main about state formation. She refers to the state-building processes at work in years like 1776, 1789, 1830 and 1848, just like Moyn (both also invoke lesser-known documents such as the Virginia Declaration of Rights [1776], setting precedents for more famous later episodes). Also like Moyn, "abstract principles" were invoked in such processes. For Hunt, "declaring rights," be it in France, America or the 1804 declaration of independence in Haiti, was a matter of those abstract principles and their cultural momentum. The idea of political participation without limitation would eventually "come home to roost" in full, unabridged form (Hunt 2007, 153). Built on top of cultures of "inherence," documents like the French and American Declarations allowed "no exceptions" to political participation for those who "fulfilled the age and economic conditions of eligibility" (Hunt 2007, 153). "All-inclusiveness" would need work. Hunt's more than aware of that. It was a principle, however, on which twentieth-century international rights would be instituted, and further work could be done to realize at least some of their promise.

Still, agreement with Moyn on this point also represents the point at which he and Hunt depart ways. Taking a more contextualist approach, Moyn again asserts that the "rights of man" or *droits de l'homme* were really not *humanity*'s rights. The gesture towards the full recognition of *all* individuals' rights was empty as internationalism generally wasn't present on the eighteenth-century political agenda. Indeed, all the way through the 1940s – even the 1950s and '60s – when ethnic minorities, women or the poor petitioned for rights, it was almost *always* as citizens. Again, there are arguments to be made for this. When the American Congress passed the fifteenth amendment, however (barring race as a barrier to voting), this was *purely* in the context of the state; it was an American issue. The same might be said of the range of European and North American states granting women the franchise in the years surrounding the First World War (Adams 2014). Hunt doesn't deny this point. She's clear on the idea that the UN regime and regimes derived from it would expand rights in ways Enlightenment predecessors could only imagine – and perhaps didn't. Still, rights have nowhere to go conceptually without inherence – they go nowhere without the *comprehension* of inherence – and that, in any systematic way, is a notion emerging in the eighteenth century. It's a distinct dating for rights. For Hunt (2007, 205), the UN regime "crystallized 150 years of struggle for [rights]." Rights' concrete roots came in the throes of democratic revolution and the largely French and North American vocabularies fostering new-birthed democracies to which a longer history of rights would respond.

Lauren: The Ancient Rider

I indicated in the introduction that the foil for all this is Lauren's book – *Visions Seen: The Evolution of International Human Rights* – and it's true. Published in 1998, Lauren's work was part of a wave of publications emerging during to the Universal Declaration's fifty-year anniversary (e.g., Montgomery 1999; van der Heijden and Tahzib 1998). It was celebrated as such. There were good reasons to do so. Up to that point, rights *qua* field was relatively dominated by lawyers and political scientists (see Freeman 2011). Leading questions were often either determining what rights were (how does one know one has them?), their legal dimensions or how rights would be applied or used (how do we get them to people who should have them? [see Freeman 2011]). Due in part to the popularity of the idea – that, as Moyn indicates, rights may be the "last utopia" – we now expect rights to involve historical analysis and discussions of cultural significance. Previous to the '90s this was rarely so. Lauren's book was an articulation of a history long presumed but little told.

Still, Lauren's title is revealing. "Visions," and "visionary men and women" (Lauren 2003, 1) is the theme. This means those who had the capacity "to see beyond the confines of what is or what has been, and to creatively dream or imagine what might be." What might be, of course, was human rights. One reviewer in *The International History Review* (Merrills 1999, 1122) ascribes this as Lauren's "main strength" as well as his "principle weakness." The strength is that Lauren tells a story many want – the idea that many of us think rights and that more than a few souls look for the freedom rights embody. The weakness, however (again, Merrills 1999, 1122), is "leaving the reader with

the impression that the thinkers of an earlier age were struggling, with varying degrees of success, to express ideas which we now take for granted." It's
a good point. Lauren's history is goal-centered. Historically, rights are, or at
least have been, what they claim to be: "inherent" and "inalienable" (United
Nations 1948, preamble). A little part of us, even if it's not always explainable,
has supposedly always known or sensed the essence of rights.

Lauren's tack is simple. Moving far beyond the Enlightenment, he memo-
rializes the visionaries "in many different times, places, and circumstances"
who helped others "enjoy freedom, dignity and the protection of their fundamental rights." He tells an international history; there's no presumption that
liberal ideas and political freedom are purely Western concepts. No "single
society, political system, culture, geographical region, or manner" is responsible for rights, Lauren maintains (2003, 2). Ideas suggesting such notions,
Lauren believes, are artifacts of enormous presumption. They miss a more
global narrative emerging when one backlights human rights in more than
one hue.

Now, it should be said that Lauren's focus is the post-Enlightenment period.
By "post-Enlightenment," I mean not just the Romantic Age following the
Enlightenment, but the entire swath of nineteenth- and twentieth-century
history leading us to the situations we have today. Post-Enlightenment rights
are broad: William Wilberforce and the abolitionists, the increasing adoption
of anti-slavery laws, Christian humanitarians, activists for women's rights, artists like Eugène Delacroix embodying freedom through works such as "Liberty Leading the People" (1830), India's anti-caste *Ramakrishna* movement,
the Chartist Movement, Marxism, the Paris Commune, the founding of the
Red Cross, Sultan Abdulmejid's 1839 proclamation of *Hatti-I Sherif* (protecting religious minorities in the Ottoman Empire), Talibov-I Tabrizi's exposi-
tions on individual rights, the foundation of the NAACP and of course the
establishment of early rights NGOs such as the *Ligue des Droits de l'Homme*
(1898). As Lauren portrays it, momentum built through the torsions of the
First World War and attempts to ameliorate that conflict's effects. The League
of Nations was a failed attempt at international rights. Still, they were in discourse, and arguing otherwise either ignores the facts or ideas so alike it's less
than meaningful to pretend otherwise.

For Lauren, the centerpiece is nonetheless World War II. I say "nonetheless"
since, as Etinson notes in his review of Moyn, World War II is often taken as
important regardless of how old one thinks rights are. The Second World
War and post-Holocaust activism are frequently pointed to turning points

in the history of rights (Ishay 2004; Morsink 1999) and it appears that more than a few involved in drafting the Universal Declaration at least rhetorically referred to the War and its tragedies in the process (see also Normand and Zaidi 2008). Indeed, the Universal Declaration and the Convention on the Prevention and Punishment of the Crime of Genocide (1948) were passed by the UN General Assembly within a day of one another. John Humphrey, the Canadian lawyer so central for the Universal Declaration in fact had a hand in both (Normand and Zaidi 2008). As Lauren sees it, the War crystallized an increasingly democratic and liberational sentiment making it a "people's" war. Mass mobilization – well beyond the First World War – forced a clear articulation of goals. Documents like the Atlantic Charter (1941), Franklin Roosevelt's 1941 State of the Union Address (addressing his famous "Four Freedoms") and the "Declaration by United Nations" from the 1941–2 Arcadia Conference were significant.[5] These used human rights to elevate their rhetoric, and provide a cause that at least *might* transcend national bounds. By 1942, quoting the Declaration by United Nations (not to be confused with a "Declaration *of* the United Nations"), liberal powers together with the Soviets declared their interest to "to preserve human rights and justice in their own lands as well as in other lands" (Yale Law School 2008). Human rights should provide freedom from fear, want, freedom of worship and freedom of speech (Roosevelt's notion). For Lauren, neither the Universal Declaration nor subsequent rights treaties and declarations were easy wins. Massive NGO and activist effort was devoted to making rights appear in the UN Charter and, moreover, that the Charter would lead to a rights declaration and concrete set of international rights treaties (the Declaration, together with the International Covenant on Civil and Political Rights [1966] and the International Covenant on Economic, Social and Cultural Rights [1966] are the foundations of the UN system).[6] Still, the "people's war" birthed a "people's peace" (Lauren 2003, 165). Again, though no win would be easy, a new era was upon us.

These are meaningful points. Few dispute that, regardless of when one sees it as having happened, it was *sometime* in the twentieth century that rights gained a full head of steam. There's more reference to rights in the twentieth century than before. Still, it's the opening chapter in Lauren's book

---

5 Before the U.S. Congress, Roosevelt (1941) asked for "freedom of speech and expression," "freedom of every person to worship God in his own way," "freedom from want" and "freedom from fear" – often pointed to as loosely outlining the principles of international human rights (see Ishay 2004, 212).

6 See United Nations (1996).

that provokes the most interest. Entitled "My Brother's and Sister's Keeper: Visions and the Origins of Human Rights," Lauren locates the earliest overtures to rights in places fully avoided by Hunt and Moyn: worlds of early moral thought cutting across several pre-modern cultures and encompassing enough belief systems such that few are left out. It's provocative. Though he includes Greco-Roman law (2008, 14) in its early outlines of republicanism and natural law, the point is religious belief. "In Hinduism," Lauren (2003, 6) asserts, "...the ancient texts of the Vedas and Upanishads...stress that divine truth is universal, that life is sacred [and] ... the virtues of tolerance and compassion ... justice and moral action." Judaism did the same. Leviticus, Lauren (2003, 7) points out, admonishes that "you shall not oppress; you shall not do injustice; you shall love your neighbor as yourself." Buddhism, embodied in Siddhartha's teachings (Lauren 2003, 8), attacked the Hindu caste system. People of "all caste and rank" should become members of "one and the same society." Eventually, Christians, Confucianists and Muslims jumped on the bandwagon. They took world as it "is" (Lauren 2003, 10) and devised directives to how it "should be." They asked us to "turn the other cheek." They asked us to give *zakat* (Muslim alms-giving) and find heavenly "virtue" (Confucianism). "Moral imperatives," Lauren (2003, 10) suggests, are the heart of rights. "Human responsibility to others," embodied in most major religions and social philosophies, is indispensable. Here, the cultural hold of rights knows no geographical boundaries. Many political and ethical systems incorporate rights. Rights also acknowledge no *historical* boundaries. They're old. Roughly, rights coincide with the history of civilization itself.

Now, I said I'd avoid discussion of "intellectual history," or what a history of ideas properly "is." I'll beat a quiet retreat. In his 1969 article "Meaning and Understanding in the History of Ideas," intellectual historian Quentin Skinner (40) warned of attempting to read backwards into ideas, or imbue words evoked in contexts other than our own with the meanings *we* have in mind. "An understanding of any idea," Skinner argued, "requires an understanding of all the occasions and activities in which a given agent might have used all the relevant form of words." Texts involve "oblique strategies." They're opaque and grounded. Discourses are hard to see through. Ideas are the same. They're not easily read and, ripped from context, they lose meaning. J.G. Merrills (1999, 1123), in his *The International History Review* examination of Lauren's work picks up on this. Rights are ideas "we now take for granted." We use concepts and mean particular things when we do. We have a circle of ideas around rights concepts. Those ideas may be different, however, than

---

the "complex intellectual world" (here I intersperse Skinner's vocabulary) of the *alternate* eras in which Lauren's visionaries operated. E.g., if both sought to do "good," did Siddhartha (ancient moralist) and Eleanor Roosevelt (twentieth-century rights activist) really mean the same thing? Was the founder of Buddhism's good *precisely* the same as that of an early twentieth-century pioneer for international justice? Was morality in northeast India in the fifth and sixth centuries BCE the same as morality in North America and Europe, where the bulk of the concrete work on human rights was done? Hard to say. What seems fair to say is they were vastly different circumstances in vastly different times.

Indeed, this points to a problem in Lauren's work generally: not only that the historical meanings might be different, but that rights being a point of contest *today* might reflect the impossibility of coincidences of meaning at-large. Few (see Risse, Ropp and Sikkink 1999) suggest that rights "become" popular and societies simply "adopt" them. More than a little pressure and negotiation is needed for rights to expand and they are often taken as a norm as opposed to a "natural" belief. Rights are often posed as relative. Today, notions of "Asian Values" and "Islamic" rights concepts abound. As Singaporean Prime Minister Lee Kwan Yew (1992) put it, what non-Westerners value, "may not ... be what Americans or Europeans value." Indeed, cultural relativism was a battle upon the initial adoption of human rights. The level of individual independence embodied in the Universal Declaration, Saudi representative Jamil Baroody maintained (in Morsink 1999, 21), took into account "only the standards recognized by Western civilization." "Ancient civilizations which were past the experimental stage, and the institutions of which ... had proved their wisdom through the centuries" were ignored. Baroody's example was marriage – a point on which UN rights were liberal, but the Muslim societies for which Baroody spoke (especially in 1948) were not. The meaning of culture in rights is a still still-unfolding battle in the space of international politics.[7]

This may not prove Lauren "wrong." Ideas concern definitions, and if rights can be defined as "good" or "sympathy" – and perhaps they can – he may be onto something. Rights involve more than a little moralism. *Comprehending* Lauren's thesis is another matter, however. Largely due to his book's first chapter, Lauren is clear: predating the Enlightenment – certainly predating 1948 or the 1970s – human rights are an ancient concept. Human rights con-

---

7 See also An-Na'im (1992), addressing a wide variety of the problems concerning intercultural concord over rights.

cern dissatisfaction with the world as it is and a "determination to make it as it *ought to be*" (Lauren 2003, 6). À la Hunt, "ought to be" involves sympathy and compassion. One recognizes the difficulties that most human beings have as well as their essential similarities. For Lauren, though, Georgian portraiture and epistolary novels like Richardson's *Clarissa* didn't lead to such recognition. Nor did 1970s embraces of Eastern Bloc dissidents or problems in Vietnam. Recognition was a practice societies had been involved in for millennia. It is as old as philosophy and law themselves. As such – natural to the human being – recognition is a process societies might refine, or continue to develop, for millennia into the future.

History and Policy: Dating Ideas, Placing Ourselves

In the introduction, I said I use a weak sense of "intellectual history," and it's true. Certainly, I'm not pointing to "unit-ideas," as did Arthur O. Lovejoy in his 1936 *The Great Chain of Being: The Study of the History of an Idea*. In this seminal book, the founding editor of the *Journal of the History of Ideas* suggested that "unit-ideas" were the component parts of larger philosophical concepts that were arranged and rearranged to make yet more concepts through time. Of these, Lovejoy (2009, 4) thought there were relatively few. I can't say what the component parts of "human rights" would be beyond "human" and "rights." I'd suggest we approach the idea as an intuitive whole as much as a philosophical notion we dissect with precision. As Moyn (2010, 1) notes, human rights may be an "ideal" – a sensibility and intuition as much as anything else. That we don't know if we're talking about law, morality, definitions that have clarity or not may assist to confusion over when rights "start."

Still, I'm not sure "human rights" are but words with meanings. Yes, as a Skinnerian approach would imply, we have to utter "human rights." We have many forms of the vocabulary, and they need to be detected. Ideas and statements shouldn't be taken out of context. Still, it's a problem for a Skinner-like perspective that we sometimes have to work across many languages, and an entire fabric of social usage, especially of a concept with global play, is hard to put together. Perhaps one could fall back on the changes in meanings of concepts, as did Reinhart Koselleck (1972) and colleagues in their *Begriffsgeschichte* project, where a particular concept (as opposed to unit ideas) underwent social transformation. As Jeremy Rayner (1988, 497) notes in his criticism of *Begriffsgeschichte*, however, this brings heavy assumptions about "family" resemblances – that likenesses exist to be found even though concepts supposedly change. Maybe one might look for *mentalités*, like the

Annales School of the 1970s and '80s – "cohesion of systems of thought" in socio-economic context (in Gismondi 1985, 211). As any Annales historian would tell you, however, that is a massive task. It relies on "total histories" perhaps not possible. The problem with putting on a methodologically tight suit of is that one has to wear the clothes. It's tough to go around in pants a size too small.

Still, we can see conceptual problems – conceptual-*historical* problems – in human rights. Scholars take positions on the idea – positions concerning the naturalness of rights, points of its rhetorical development, the ways in which that development took place – and make those positions fundamental. "Origins" seem to determine all. It's funny; neither Moyn nor Hunt explicitly name Lauren, nor anyone else for that matter, as offering the "standard" history of human rights. The "church history," as Moyn (2010, 8) again poses it, is but *presumed* to exist. Again, that presumption isn't unreasoned. Rights present *themselves* as a progressive history. Perhaps that's necessary. It can be hard to convince governments and populations of ideas if they're not posed as "natural," "inevitable" or connected to the "nature" of who we are. In their collection on political thought, e.g., Michael Rosen and Jonathan Wolff (1999, 3) suggest that most ideologies build off of assertions of "what are human beings like." Theories of "humanity" underlie politics. In the 1930s, Karl Mannheim (1985, 122) pointed out that ideology is connected to "utopia." Political schemes concern visions of the future. "Utopia," however, is based on arguments concerning its realization – that "it can be shown there is an interrelationship between events and configurations [of experiences] through which everything, by virtue of its position acquires significance." It's hard to imagine rights *not* connecting themselves to human nature and senses that they've been here since time immemorial, or that they're matters of "fact" as much as "theory." "Church history," Moyn – and to some extent Hunt – seem to say, almost needn't be written. It's among us. It's supposed.

Still, someone wrote the church history, and if "standard history," at least of rights, is a church, Lauren is the deacon. Lauren's work is serious. Richard Pierre Claude, founding editor of *Human Rights Quarterly* (1999, 252), called *The Evolution of International Human Rights* "beautiful," and he's right. It's a vast, crafted work covering large historical distances and incorporating impressive levels of knowledge. "A finer gift on the fiftieth anniversary of the Universal Declaration of Human Rights," wrote Natalie Kaufman (2000, 898) in her *The American Historical Review* review, is difficult to imagine. It's a large book; it articulates the stories we expect yet haven't always been told.

We need this. We need meat on the bone of the story we imagine and the self-definitions we have. Lauren puts that there.

Still, his *is* a teleological history. Useful or not, Lauren looks to *advance* human rights and support them as much as anything else. Again, decisive is Lauren's primordial sense of religion. Descending into pasts thousands of years old, Lauren portrays religion as embodying rights' impulse – justice, universality and the desire for a better world. Rights are essentially ethical challenges for personal and social improvement. It's a point giving rights activists hope their message might be understood. If the essence of rights could be thought in the past – and to the cross-cultural degree Lauren poses – it could be thought *now*. Again, using Lauren's (2003, 2) vocabulary, rights come from no "single society, political system, culture, geographical region, or manner." That they belong to no one means they belong to all. It's a message rights activists want to hear.

Hunt is more tepid about this possibility. Yes, rights played out in non-European and non-North American locales as liberal ideas and socialist offshoots took hold in the developing world and the periphery of empires. However, if not in the space of specifically Anglophone and French philosophy, it's certainly within the sinews of a world *derived* from Euro-American thought that rights emerged. Nationalism, socialism, anti-colonialism and the women's movement, Hunt notes, all drew succor from the discourses of Enlightenment. That indicates rights as a global affair across the nineteenth and twentieth centuries. It also indicates them, however, as having eighteenth-century "Western" roots regardless of who adopted them or not. It challenges Lauren's argument and potentially narrows the scope of rights' appeal.

Moyn goes the furthest regarding human rights' conceptual limitations. Again, 1948 is the breaking point. Before 1948, few politicians, organizations or states discussed rights in ways intended to cross national borders and establish *inter*national regimes of social norms and systems of justice. Indeed, even during World War II (Moyn 2010, 49), statements like the Arcadia Conference's "Declaration by United Nations" or Atlantic Charter's, in which rights were invoked, were relatively rare. It was "undoubtedly a heroic achievement of diplomatic consensus" that the Universal Declaration passed through the UN General Assembly, Moyn (2010, 68) rights. That heroism was forgotten, though, until civil society activists reinvigorated a form of it in the late '60s and '70s. Moyn sees rights – *human* rights – as an idea with borders. They can't be posited particularly far outside the dimensions of the UN, and concrete discourses deriving from the UN Charter, the Universal Declaration and other basic rights documents are where, in fact, rights are to be found.

What concerns me is a bit less the *type* of intellectual history used to discuss rights than the idea that there are implications for the results of the intellectual-historical arguments invoked by scholars *regardless* of approach. Again, Lauren is the rights supporter *par excellence*. Organizations such as Amnesty and Human Rights Watch and supranational organizations like the UN need histories like his. Pro-rights actors have to muster *some* level of evidence that the ideas they seek aren't just *their* ideas – imposed imaginations of intellectuo-political elites. One can poo-poo "Whiggish," or self-serving, histories of rights. They might be facile and triumphalist. Rights movements are diverse, though. They haven't been and aren't just advanced by educated Westerners, and massive ranges of grass roots activists in broad stripes of global locales have sought regional and international attention on issues from HIV (a large issue in sub-Saharan Africa) to unjust imprisonment (Cuba's *damas de blanco*, for example) (see Quataert 2011b; Madison 2010) to the multiple modes of activism leading to the recent take off in LGBT rights (also highly global). In part, that may concern at least *claimed* histories of rights transcending the 1970s, 1940s, or perhaps the borders of the West.[8]

Again, Hunt and Moyn trouble this idea. Roughly, Hunt's position can be equated with what Jack Donnelly's (2007, 284–85) terms the "relative universality" of human rights. Here, Donnelly's claim echoes Hunt's: "no society, civilization, or culture prior to the seventeenth century … had a widely endorsed practice, or even vision, of equal and unalienable individual human rights." Now, Donnelly uses an expansive view of the Enlightenment – a rough view of an increasingly progressivist eighteenth century debated by Enlightenment scholars (see Israel 2001) yet deployed by figures like Hunt (2007, 60). Still, he underlines the importance of this philosophy. Again, important is that rights *become* universal. They spread through Europe. They then spread to the world. That's as *norms*, though. That's as *inculcated* practices. One has to be acculturated to rights. They're *not* natural to all. That's a cautionary tale for rights institutions and movements as they evoke claims to "natural" political acts in the name of "all" humankind.

Moyn straightjackets the idea. Though he's critical of the United Nations, the UN was successful in forming the vision of rights from which most rights

---

8 I simply point here to the idea that establishing rights legacies in the present may involve interpretation of the past, including multiple culture's sense of relatedness to the concept. See Campbell and Penna (1998).

organizations and rights-interested activists would operate. In his portrayal, rights become a popular vocabulary through grass roots movements and their pragmatic appropriation international politics. The conceptual touchstone nonetheless remains the UN. Again, whether Amnesty International or the Helsinki process, it was the Universal Declaration explicitly named as the fount of rights concepts ("in the field of human rights and fundamental freedoms, the participating States will act in conformity with the purposes and principles of the Charter of the United Nations and with the Universal Declaration of Human Rights," wrote the Conference on Security and Cooperation in Europe in the Helsinki Accords [1975] – but one example).[9] Here, while rights are a utopian concept – an "ideal" of the "highest moral precepts" (Moyn 2010, 1) – there's a letter to the law. Stray too far from the specific vocabularies outlined in the Universal Declaration and subsequent UN conventions, and one's no longer discussing human rights. There's little room for debate about what rights are or whether one is living up to them.

This is where the rubber hits the road. We *use* rights. UN Security Council (2011; 2014) resolutions are used to justify NATO intervention in places like Libya and Syria. Rights are talking points in great power dances between Europe, the U.S., China and Russia as they negotiate over issues like the Ukraine, freedom of information, economic challenges and liberties for gay and queer communities. Human rights enter states – powerful states like the U.S. – as figures like Bernie Sanders propose European-style models of health care extending well beyond Obama's Affordable Care Act (Wagner 2015). Issues of citizenship and statelessness confront Europe as refugees with varying statuses emigrate from conflict in Africa and the Middle East and ask Western states to open their doors. Dimensions of free speech have been challenged in the wake of Paris and Copenhagen shootings where the question is whether expression can be absolute, or if it needs to reign itself for intercultural concord. Fourteen and a half percent of the world lives on under $1.25 a day – the measure of extreme poverty (World Bank Group 2015) and a right in absolutely no one's book. These are well-covered phenomena (Iacobucci and Toope 2015; Rubio-Marín 2014). They also bring no easy answers. Can one defend rights down the barrel of a gun? Are civil liberties in one place to be the same as those in others? Need we be concerned with double

---

9 Almost all regional rights regimes depart from the Universal Declaration as well – the European Convention on Human Rights (1950), the American Convention on Human Rights (1969), the African Charter on Human and Peoples' Rights (1981) and even the Arab Charter of Human Rights (2004) and the ASEAN Human Rights Declaration. See Shelton and Carozza (2013).

standards in rights, and are rights a generalized humanitarian sentiment or concrete sets of laws? Some say yes, some say no. There are many pragmatic politics to make around rights. Regardless of how one views such issues, however, there's a question of what one is doing – or, perhaps, what one *thinks* one is doing – when one invokes human rights as a standard one *might* use and to which all, in some capacity, *could* conform. Is one holding out absolutes? Is one insisting on universals? Is one asking for more than we can achieve? Or does one have something more relative in mind? In the wake of *Charlie Hebdo*, the UN Human Rights Commissioner (United Nations News Center 2015) was quick to offer his condemnation. In contradistinction of principles of free speech, Zeid Ra'ad al Hussein suggested – never mind problems of intercultural concord – the January shootings were "appalling and ruthless." They fed "discrimination and prejudice" – two concepts opposed to rights. They contradicted incontrovertible and baseline absolutes. In the "age of rights," as Bobbio (1996) formulated, we have standards. Sometimes those are negotiated. They sometimes involve compromise. Sometimes not, though. Often, rights are assumed as "there," and concepts all should recognize.

What intellectual history does is both support this and not. The evidence that particular standards are "there" becomes more forceful when the people for whom those standards are supposed to be "real" (all of us) assent to them. Lauren argues that rights abuses invariably occur. Activists have "visions" because the world *is* as it is, and it *hasn't* been sufficiently improved. We haven't *always* been "my brother's keeper," as he puts it, and we've let each other down. The resources to combat problems come not from a particular time and place, but humanity *itself*. This, however, is why we need to note the impact of "prophets, philosophers, and activists" far "transcend[ing] our own time and place" (Lauren 2003, 1). Rights are absolute. There's a need to somehow inform those who don't "get it" what the truth in fact is. Evidence for that absoluteness comes from a larger view of human history.

Hunt limits this claim. Rights transcended twentieth- and twenty-first-century worlds and didn't stay within the West. However, we inculcated and developed rights through "cultures." "Cultures" might not always look like eighteenth-century Europe and America. Theoretically, "empathy" and "autonomy" aren't limited to Britain, the U.S., France, Germany or any other Western state. A particular intellectual and semiotic dissemination nonetheless has to take place. Without social reinforcement making rights intuitive, they don't enter "minds" (Hunt 2007, 34). Without social transmission, rights lack presence and have the potential to fall on deaf ears. It's a world Hunt doesn't want. It can happen, though, when rights aren't automatically universal – which, if they're so closely bound to one culture (the Enlightenment West), they are potentially not.

For Moyn, rights – again, *human* rights – might not be "there" at all. The level of specificity one is involved with human rights is so high that for the world to realize rights, one has to become quite insistent on inculcating a very particular regime. Again, that's UN-based as it's there the essence of rights lies. That vindicates rights' essential vision – they *should* to know no boundary in terms of effectiveness or meaning. It also offers a sinister sense, however, of what's at work when one insists on rights or suggests power should be used in their name. It becomes insistence and imposition. It becomes *telling* others what rights should be. Yes, the UN "debates" rights. They're argued over. Only within certain parameters, though. Outside of those parameters, rights aren't "rights" anymore. They're something else, not deserving of the name.

For what my own voice is worth here, I find Lauren less than convincing. "Good," "care" or "sympathy" and "human rights" may not ultimately be equitable – that as I might reject human rights but think it "good," or "beneficial" to do so. That's not a matter of insisting on the value of one cultural community over another. It's a simply a recognition that universal rights are complex and one may need to modulate them for consensus to emerge. Moyn is convincing regarding human rights' international quality. It's an open question whether French or American revolutionaries had UN rights in mind (they most likely did not), and there's little question international rights had lesser conceptual life before the UN and the slow bubble of rights into the space of global social consciousness. Still, the French wrote "men are born and remain free and equal in rights" and that rights are "natural, inalienable and sacred," and others, especially the Americans, produced documents with similar rings. The lawyers, politicians and philosophers working on the Universal Declaration in the 1940s wrote that "all human beings are born free and equal in dignity and rights" and one should have access to the "equal and inalienable rights of the human family." The similarities are hard to ignore. That leaves me in the vicinity of Hunt. We need to recognize both the abstract vocabularies as well as the specific institutional settings in which human rights emerge. Rights are always contextual and most certainly not ahistorical. When one says, as the authors of the Universal Declaration seemed to, that a particular set of vocabularies has been influential, I'm simply not sure why one wouldn't take them at their word. It doesn't make "revolutionary rights" the same as the UN's. It might make them darn close, though.

In the end, though, my argument here is nothing more or less here than that such debates matter. As exemplified by Moyn, Hunt and Lauren, efforts to tell the history of an idea, regardless of how skeptical one is towards it, elucidates the thinking of politics, policy and the arguments made to support them. It also elucidates, from time to time, what one might say to degrade the role of rights in political space (i.e., narrower views of rights might lead to more limited uses of the concept). Histories of concepts tell us how culturally translatable particular policies might be – from the optimistic readings of such issues (Lauren) to the relatively pessimistic (Moyn). For a small area within the larger space of rights – the attempt to tell their intellectual history – that's a charge with a lot of power. It's an analytical task with a lot of oomph. Intellectual history reveals the thoughtways under rights discourses and opens dimensions of their argumentation often accepted, but nonetheless left unsaid. I wonder: Where's my *Town and Country*? Shouldn't I have an intellectual history journal beside it?

Refernences

Adams, Jad. 2014. *Women and the Vote: A World History.* Oxford: Oxford University Press.

Afshari, Reza. 2007. "On the Historiography of Human Rights: Reflections on Paul Gordon Lauren's 'The Evolution of International Human Rights: Visions Seen.'" *Human Rights Quarterly* 29 (1): 1–67.

Andreopoulos, George, and Zehra F. Kabasakal Arat, eds. 2014. *The Uses and Misuses of Human Rights: A Critical Approach to Advocacy.* New York: Palgrave.

An-Na'im, Abdullahai, ed. 1992. *Human Rights in Cross-Cultural Perspectives: A Quest for Consensus.* Philadelphia: University of Pennsylvania Press.

Aune, David. 2013. *Jesus, Gospel Tradition and Paul in the Context of Jewish and Greco-Roman Antiquity.* Tübingen: Mohr Siebeck.

Bietz, Charles. 2009. *The Idea of Human Rights.* Oxford: Oxford University Press.

Bobbio, Norberto. 1996. *The Age of Rights.* Trans. Allan Cameron. Cambridge: Polity.

de Bolla, Peter. 2009. "Rights and Sentiments." *History Workshop Journal* 68: 266–73.

Campbell, Patricia, and David Penna. 1998. "Human Rights and Culture: Beyond Universality and Relativism." *Third World Quarterly* 19 (1): 7–27.

Claude, Richard Pierre. 1999. Review of *The Evolution of International Human Rights: Visions Seen* by Paul Gordon Lauren. *Human Rights Quarterly* 21 (1): 251–52.

Conference on Security and Co-operation in Europe. 1975. Final Act. Accessed June 7, 2015. Available at http://www.osce.org/mc/39501?download=true

Cmiel, Kenneth. 2004. "The Recent History of Human Rights." *The American Historical Review* 109 (1): 117–35.

Donnelly, Jack. 2003. *Universal Human Rights in Theory and Practice.* Ithaca, NY: Cornell University Press.

———. 2007. "The Relative Universality of Human Rights." *Human Rights Quarterly* 29 (2): 281–306.

Dorfman, Ben. 2014. "Are Human Rights a Philosophy of History?: The Case for the Defense." *International Social Science Review* 89 (1): 1–35.

Douzinas, Costas. 2000. *The End of Human Rights: Critical Thought at the Turn of the Century.* Oxford: Hart.

DW. 2015. "Egyptian President El-Sissi Condemned for 'Flagrant Human Rights Abuses' in First Year." Accessed June 10, 2015. Available at http://

www.dw.de/egyptian-president-el-sissi-condemned-for-flagrant-human-rights-abuses-in-first-year/a-18504067.

Ellis, Ralph. 2014. "UN to Investigate Alleged Human Rights Abuses by ISIS." *CNN*. Accessed June 10, 2015. Available at http://edition.cnn.com/2014/09/01/world/meast/iraq-crisis/.

Etinson, Adam. 2012. Review of *The Last Utopia: Human Rights in History* by Samuel Moyn. *Human Rights Quarterly* 34 (1): 294–99.

Foucault, Michel. 1977. *Language, Counter-Memory, Practice: Selected Essays and Interviews by Michel Foucault*. Edited by Donald F. Bouchard. Ithaca, NY: Cornell University Press.

Freeman, Michael. 2011. *Human Rights: An Interdisciplinary Approach*. Cambridge: Polity.

Gismondi, Michael A. 1985. "'The Gift of Theory': A Critique of the histoire des mentalités." *Social History* 10 (2): 211–30.

Hunt, Lynn. 2007. *Inventing Human Rights: A History*. New York: W.W. Norton.

Iacobucci, Edward M., and Stephen J. Toope. 2015. *After the Paris Attacks: Responses in Canada, Europe and Around the Globe*. Toronto: University of Toronto Press.

Ignatieff, Michael. 2000. *The Rights Revolution*. Toronto: House of Anansi Press.

———. 2001. *Human Rights as Politics and Idolatry*. Princeton: Princeton University Press.

Ishay, Micheline R. 2004. *The History of Human Rights: From Ancient Times to the Globalization Era*. Berkeley: University of California Press.

Israel, Jonathan. 2001. *Radical Enlightenment: Philosophy and the Making of Modernity, 1650–1750*. Oxford: Oxford University Press.

———. 2011. *Democratic Enlightenment: Philosophy, Revolution, and Human Rights 1750–1790*. Oxford: Oxford University Press.

Jarrell, Randall. 1954. *Pictures from an Institution: A Comedy*. New York: Knopf.

Kammerhoffer, Jörg. 2012. "Orthodox Generalists and Political Activists in International Legal Scholarship." In *International Law in Multipolar World*, edited by Matthew Happold, 138–57. London: Routledge.

Kant, Immanuel. 2006a. "An Answer to the Question 'What is Enlightenment?'" In *Towards Perpetual Peace and Other Writings on Peace, Politics, and History*. Translated by Pauline Kleingeld, 17–23. New Haven: Yale University Press.

———. 2006b. "Towards Perpetual Peace." In *Towards Perpetual Peace and*

Other Writings on Peace, Politics, and History. Translated by Pauline Kleingeld, 67–109. New Haven: Yale University Press.

Kaufman, Natalie Hevener. 2000. Review of *The Evolution of International Human Rights: Visions Seen* by Paul Gordon Lauren. *The American Historical Review* 105 (3): 898–99.

Kelley, Donald R. 1990. "What is Happening to the History of Ideas?" *Journal of the History of Ideas* 51 (1): 3–25.

———. 2002. *The Descent of Ideas: The History of Intellectual History*. Burlington: Ashgate.

Koselleck, Reinhart. 1972. *Begriffsgeschichte und Sozialgeschichte*. In *Soziologie und Sozialgeschichte*, edited by Peter Christian Ludz, 116–31. Dordrecht: Springer.

Laslett, Peter. 1965. *The World We Have Lost*. London: Metheun.

Lauren, Paul Gordon. 2003. *The Evolution of International Human Rights: Visions Seen*. 2nd ed. Philadelphia: University of Pennsylvania Press.

Lawrence, Benjamin N. 2010. Review of *Inventing Human Rights: A History* by Lynn Hunt. *Journal of World History* 21 (2): 339–41.

Lovejoy, Arthur O. 2009. *The Great Chain of Being: A Study of the History of an Idea*. New Brunswick: Transaction.

Madison, D. Soyini. 2010. *Acts of Activism: Human Rights as Radical Performance*. Cambridge: Cambridge University Press.

Mannheim, Karl. 1985. *Ideology and Utopia*. Translated by Louis Wirth. London: Routledge.

Martin, Jean-Clément. 2008. Review of *Inventing Human Rights* by Lynn Hunt. *Annales historiques de la Révolution française* 351: 216–18.

Merrills, J.G. 1999. Review of *The Evolution of International Human Rights: Visions Seen* by Paul Gordon Lauren and *NGOs and the Universal Declaration of Human Rights: "A Curious Grapevine"* William Korey. *The International History Review* 21 (4): 1121–23.

Montgomery, John D. 1999. "Fifty Years of Human Rights: An Emergent Global Regime." *Political Sciences* 32 (1): 79–94.

Morsink, Johannes. 1999. *The Universal Declaration of Human Rights: Origins, Drafting & Intent*. Philadelphia: University of Pennsylvania Press.

Moyn, Samuel. 2010. *The Last Utopia: Human Rights in History*. Cambridge, MA: Harvard Belknap.

Moyn, Samuel and Jan Eckel, eds. 2013. *The Breakthrough: Human Rights in the 1970s*. Philadelphia: University of Pennsylvania Press.

Myers, Stephen Lee and Eric Schmitt. 2013. "Obama Urged to Prod China at Rights at Meeting." *The New York Times*. Accessed June 10, 2015. Available at http://www.nytimes.com/2013/06/07/world/asia/obama-urged-to-prod-china-on-human-rights.html?_r=0.

Normand, Roger and Sarah Zaidi. 2008. *Human Rights at the UN: The Politics of Universal Justice*. Bloomington: Indiana University Press.

Palmer, R.R. 2014. *The Age of Democratic Revolution*. Princeton: Princeton University Press.

Quataert, Jean H. 2011a. Review of *The Last Utopia: Human Rights in History* by Samuel Moyn. *The English Historical Review* 126 (521): 1028–29.

———. 2011b. *Advocating Dignity: Human Rights Mobilizations in Global Politics*. Philadelphia: University of Pennsylvania Press.

Rawls, John. 1993. *Political Liberalism*. New York: Columbia University Press.

Rayner, Jeremy. 1988. "On Begriffsgeschichte." *Political Theory* 16 (3): 496–501.

Risse, Thomas, Stephen C. Ropp and Kathryn Sikkink, eds. 1999. *The Power of Human Rights: International Norms and Domestic Change*. Cambridge: Cambridge University Press.

Roosevelt, Franklin. 1941. Message to Congress. Accessed June 12, 2015. Available at http://www.fdrlibrary.marist.edu/pdfs/ffreadingcopy.pdf.

Rosen, Michael and Jonathan Wolff, eds. 1999. *Political Thought*. Oxford: Oxford University Press.

Rorty, Amélia Oksenberg. 1996. "Descartes and Spinoza on Epistemological Egalitarianism." *History of Philosophy Quarterly* 13 (1): 35–53.

Rousseau, Jean-Jacques. 1969. *The Social Contract*. Translated by Maurice Cranston. New York: Penguin.

Rubio-Marín, Ruth, ed. 2014. *Human Rights and Immigration*. Oxford: Oxford University Press.

Shelton, Dinah, and Paola Carozza, eds. 2013. *Regional Protection of Human Rights, vol. 1*. Oxford: Oxford University Press.

Skinner, Quentin. 1969. "Meaning and Understanding in the History of Ideas." *History and Theory* 8 (1): 3–53.

Slaughter, Joseph. 2007. *Human Rights Inc.: The World Novel, Narrative Form, and International Law*. New York: Fordham University Press.

Turner, Bryan S. 2011. "The Short History of Human Rights." *Contemporary Sociology* 46 (6): 678–80.

Turpin, Paul. 2011. *The Moral Rhetoric of Political Economy: Justice and Modern Economic Thought*. London: Routledge.

United Nations. 1948. The Universal Declaration of Human Rights. Accessed June 1, 2005. Available at http://www.un.org/en/documents/udhr/

———. 1996. Fact Sheet No. 2 (Rev. 1); The International Bill of Human Rights. Accessed June 1, 2015. Available at http://www.ohchr.org/Documents/Publications/FactSheet2Rev.1en.pdf

United Nations News Center. 2015. "Ban Outraged by 'Horrendous and Cold-Blooded Attack' on French Magazine." Access June 2, 2015. Available at http://www.un.org/apps/news/story.asp?NewsID=49741#.VXVWNs-qqko

United Nations Security Council. 2011. Resolution 1973. Accessed June 2, 2015. Available at http://www.un.org/en/ga/search/view_doc.asp?symbol=S/RES/1973(2011).

———. 2014. Resolution 2165. Accessed June 2, 2015. Available at http://www.un.org/en/ga/search/view_doc.asp?symbol=S/RES/2165(2014).

van der Heijden, Barend and Bahia Tahzib, eds. 1998. *Reflections on the Universal Declaration of Human Rights: A Fiftieth Anniversary Anthology*. The Hague: Kluwer.

Yale Law School. 2008. Declaration by United Nations. Accessed June 3, 2005. Available at http://avalon.law.yale.edu/20th_century/decade03.asp

Yew, Lee Kwan. 1992. "Democracy, Human Rights and the Realities." *Ministerial Speeches* 16 (2): 20–37.

Wagner, John. 2015. "Sanders Advocates for Single-Payer Healthcare System on Medicare Anniversary." Accessed September 30, 2015. Available at http://www.washingtonpost.com/news/post-politics/wp/2015/07/30/sanders-advocates-for-single-payer-health-care-system-on-medicare-anniversary/

Weissbrodt, David. 2008. *The Human Rights of Non-Citizens*. Oxford: Oxford University Press.

Weissbrodt, David and Connie de la Vega. 2007. *International Human Rights Law: An Introduction*. Philadelphia: University of Pennsylvania Press.

Woods, Kerri. 2014. *Human Rights*. New York: Palgrave.

World Bank Groups. 2015. *Global Monitoring Report 2014/2015*. Washington, D.C.: World Bank.

"The Holy that Has Befallen Me"
Vitalis Norström and his Intellectual Choices in a Sociology of Philosophy Perspective

Henrik Lundberg [1]

Abstract

This article examines the intellectual choices the Swedish philosopher Vitalis Norström (1856–1916) made and manifested in his seminal work *Hvad innebär en modern ståndpunkt i filosofien?* (1898). The theoretical position-taking by Norström in this text is studied through the sociological theories of intellectual choice as presented by Neil Gross, Pierre Bourdieu and Randall Collins respectively. The argument is made that the standpoints adopted by Norström are first and foremost to be understood as reflecting his self-understanding of himself as a defender and champion of the personal and rational life. Thereby, the analysis of Norström's intellectual choices in the article provides support for Gross's social-psychological theory and its theses about the influence of intellectual self-concept on such choices. It, furthermore, supports the view held by the proponents of the new sociology of ideas that macro-social factors in the first place have only an indirect influence on knowledge production. Gross's theory is, however, also criticized for failing to sufficiently clarify how strategic action and actions undertaken to remain true to one's self-concept relate to each other as explanations for intellectual choice.

In the course of the past few decades, new kind of studies have emerged that look at philosophical activity from a sociological perspective. This research has evolved under different names, among them the sociology of philosophical knowledge (Kusch 1995), the sociology of philosophy (Collins 2000), and the sociology of ideas (Camic and Gross 2001).[2] What is common to all work falling within the area, however, is the attempt made to trace philosophical thinking back to the social conditions from which it has emerged. In this article, I term this field of research the sociology of philosophy taken up as

---

1 Henrik Lundberg is senior lecturer of sociology in the Department of Sociology and Work Science at Gothenburg University.

2 For an overview of the field, see, e.g., Heidegren and Lundberg (2010).

a subdomain of the broader field of the sociology of knowledge, aspiring, through my choice of a subject matter, to contribute to the theory building in both of the areas of investigation concerned.

Within the sociology of philosophy, one of the most intriguing efforts in this latter regard has, in recent years, been Neil Gross's theory of intellectual self-concept. In his *Richard Rorty: The Making of an American Philosopher* (2008), for example, Gross has advanced the argument that, in order to explain philosophers' and intellectuals' choice of theoretical orientation, it is vital to understand their own self-understanding. As an illustration, Gross describes how Rorty's conception of himself as a "leftist American patriot' can explain why, at a certain point of his academic career, he came to embrace American pragmatism. In this article, I want to examine this argument more closely, by considering the extent to which the theory of intellectual self-concept might help us understand and explain the perspectival choices the Swedish philosopher Vitalis Norström (1856–1916) made in his seminal work *Hvad innebär en modern ståndpunkt i filosofien?* (What Is a Modern Standpoint in Philosophy? [1898]). While himself only considering thinkers working in the American academia who more or less are all of our own time, Gross, in developing his theory, was keen to point out the need for further research to test his arguments' applicability across temporal, national, cultural, and social contexts (Gross 2008, 265). One of the aims of this article is, accordingly, to examine whether the kind of social mechanisms Gross identifies as explaining Rorty's choices of intellectual perspective might also be seen as operating the same way in other periods and other sociocultural contexts, such as those producing a thinker like Norström in Sweden and the positions he took in a key theoretical text of his.

A further aim of this article is to contrast Gross's theory with two alternative theories of intellectual choice: the sociologically grounded field theories put forward by Pierre Bourdieu and Randall Collins, respectively. Gross's own work developed in an explicit polemic with both Bourdieu and Collins (see, e.g., Gross 2008, 235–63), which makes comparison between it and the type of theory represented by the latter two rather natural for anyone looking to examine and establish the validity of the theory of intellectual self-concept.[3] Given that the focus of this article is on the ability of different theories to clarify and explain how intellectual choices are made, a figure like Vitalis Norström can serve as a test case for the broader applicability of these theories

---

3 Another interesting contribution in this same area is Baert's "positioning theory" (Baert 2012).

and their theses (cf. Gross 2008, xiv). Accordingly, my discussion of Norström is not aimed at examining the validity of his arguments per se, nor does it in any way attempt to assess his significance for philosophy or his originality; his inclusion in this article serves merely a methodological purpose.

Norström's philosophy is clearly marked by its philosophy-of-life orientation. He is, however, far from the only one to have written from that perspective, even during his own time. In the course of the "long nineteenth century," many thinkers – Schopenhauer, Nietzsche, Dilthey, and Simmel merely the best known among them – came to turn against intellectualistic philosophy, to emphasize, instead, the importance of will and feelings for knowledge. Thus, what is of interest in Vitalis Norström are, in the context of this article, first and foremost his personal reasons for embracing a life-philosophical orientation, not his substantive work that was not particularly unique or ahead of his time. I will, consequently, limit myself to examining Norström's self-conception of himself as an intellectual, considering whether it might be able to yield a useful starting point for understanding his philosophical theses. Although that self-concept, as I will claim, was rooted in his personal experiences of religious nature, in doing so I will, however, no more than cursorily touch upon the question of whether Norström's own interpretation of these experiences of his might be explicable against the background of the broader cultural climate of his time. My analysis of the emergence and development of Norström's self-conception, in other words, in principle restricts itself to the influence of his personal religious experiences.

The Theory of Intellectual Self-Concept
According to the theory of intellectual self-concept as developed by Gross, intellectuals, as a rule, view themselves not just as intellectuals somehow generically, but as intellectuals of a particular type (Gross 2008, 267). Proceeding from a certain intellectual self-concept, they position themselves in cultural taxonomies, characterizing themselves as a "Marxist sociologist," a "neo-Darwinist philosopher," a "liberal political scientist," a "sociological theoretician," and so on. This self-concept then comes to shape their intellectual careers, Gross claims, with the intellectuals striving to conform to their understanding of themselves in their role as intellectuals and to realize the conception they have of themselves in their work. While the term "taxonomy" here might lead one to assume the question to be about static categories that only seldom, if ever, undergo change, this, however, is not the case. What Gross does is to weave into his theory a narrative and dynamic element that

removes this possibility (Gross 2008, 268). Just as ordinary people in society, so also intellectuals tell stories of – narrate – their intellectual lives and careers. These narratives and narrative elements serve the function of re-organizing and helping to integrate the experience intellectuals have of themselves and their work. Building on the human tendency to strive for a unified and well-integrated self-concept, they exert a causal influence on intellectuals' theoretical choices. The main motive, in other words, that drives intellectuals in their choice of theoretical standpoints is thus, if we are to believe Gross, to be found in their on-going efforts to either attain or maintain an intellectual self-concept that is at once internally coherent and congruous with their significant actions (their work).

In terms of its own intellectual orientation, the theory of intellectual self-concept has in the first place taken on two different strands of contemporary sociologically influenced thought: the traditional sociology of knowledge and its predilection for macro-social explanations on the one hand, and the position, developed more recently, that presents the choice of intellectual standpoints above all as being strategically conditioned on the other hand. The first-mentioned Gross associates primarily with Karl Mannheim and Émile Durkheim, the two founders of the sociology knowledge, but also with later writers such as Alvin Gouldner, Lewis Coser, and Robert K. Merton. The second-mentioned, to him, is most clearly represented by the work of Randall Collins and Pierre Bourdieu, both sociologists. Below, I briefly discuss these two strands of thought in this same order.

In his 2001 article "The New Sociology of Ideas," Gross and Charles Camic discuss five particular points in which the traditional sociology of knowledge in their opinion differs from what they themselves mean by their titular term. One of these concerns the extent to which macro-social factors such as social class background can explain the choices intellectuals make regarding their theoretical standpoint (Camic and Gross 2001; cf. Baert 2012, 305–309). According to the new sociology of ideas, such theoretical choices cannot in the first instance be explained by reference to general economic, cultural, or political factors and conditions; instead, the focus should lie on how small-scale, more specific meso-level circumstances such as participation in professional networks or membership in social movements can influence individuals' position-taking. Why should these meso and micro-level factors and circumstances be important for a sociological analysis of intellectuals to consider? Because, Gross explains, all that which is of interest to sociologists of knowledge unfolds in local contexts: in academic institutions, seminars, conferences, think tanks, and editorial offices and boards (Gross 2008, 11; Gross 2011, 50–51). It is in this kind of arenas that new ideas and positions are presented, criticized, met with resistance, and revised or modified. If the task of the sociology of knowledge is to gain a good understanding of individuals' intellectual activity, it, quite simply, needs to concentrate on studying the local contexts in which that activity takes place. If meso and micro level are excluded from the study of intellectuals and their work, the whole analysis is short-circuited. This, however, contrary to the objections that for instance Bryant (2011, 18) has raised against the work of Gross and the new sociologists of ideas, does nevertheless not imply disregarding macro-level conditions and processes: intellectual activity always requires as its precondition a material infrastructure that makes its being carried out possible in practice in the first place, in the form of universities, research foundations, a commercial market for the publications issuing from it, and the like. Within the sphere of the new sociology of ideas, the significance of macro-level conditions is in the first place seen as anchored in their role in the creation and shaping of, precisely, an infrastructure of this kind (Gross 2011, 51; cf. Collins 2000). The macro conditions, however, have thus admittedly no more than an indirect influence on knowledge production. In any case, what this means is that it would be a methodological error to directly relate the cognitive content of knowledge to general socio-political macro-level phenomena.

A second key respect in which Gross sees his new sociology of ideas to differ from the frameworks put forth by his predecessors concerns the claim that the choice of one's theoretical standpoint is always strategically conditioned. While it is not within the scope of this article to provide a lengthy discussion of this position, or the work, for that matter, of Bourdieu and Collins whom Gross takes up as primary representatives of it, there are a few things worth noting regarding this conception.[4] In their work, both Bourdieu and Collins engage field theories, which look at social actors in the context of their actions on a shared arena, such as, for example, the field of philosophy or sociology. The principal interest of actors in these fields, according to these theories, is to increase their status and influence within them; these two – status and power – are accorded to those who succeed in capturing their colleagues' interest and securing recognition from them. In the field of philosophy, for instance, actors orient themselves towards theories and methods that they expect can help them boost their status and enable them to achieve a posi-

---

4 For a more thorough discussion of these, see, e.g., Gross (2008), also Lundberg (2014).

tion of advantage vis-à-vis their competitors. While both Bourdieu and Collins view this strategic competition as being a fundamental characteristic of actions in the philosophical field, there is nevertheless a difference between their respective ways of understanding it. For Bourdieu (e.g., Bourdieu 1991), there is a further, even if indirect, linkage connecting philosophical position-taking to political one. In his scheme, the field of philosophy is, accordingly, for the most part characterized by a lower degree of autonomy from socio-political forces in society than in Collins's (Heidegren and Lundberg 2010; Lundberg 2014). In a way, one could say Bourdieu's work to represent a partial reflection theory: it proposes there to be a certain homology, or affinity, between positions adopted in the philosophical field and socio-political forces located outside of it. Consequently, philosophy can never completely free itself from the political context in which it is carried out or which surrounds the philosophical field.

Gross agrees that the choice of theoretical standpoints is often this way strategically motivated, as claimed by Bourdieu and Collins. What he therefore embarks upon in his own work is, as he himself makes abundantly clear, not so much aimed at refuting the latter's claims in this regard as it is at complementing the models the two have put forward (Gross 2008, 239, 264). Nevertheless, Gross is quick to point out, models of action that rely on no more than single-factor explanations for the motives behind intellectual choices, as, in his view, Bourdieu's and Collins's all too often do, can but be blind to "the richness and complexity of intellectual life"; as a result, we are presented with a view of intellectual life that is "flattened beyond recognition" (Gross 2008, 15). To be able to view intellectuals as only interested in status and power, in other words, sociologists must do violence to these intellectuals' texts and actual biographies. The cardinal error of both Bourdieu's and Collins's here is then that they both fail to adequately consider the way the intellectuals they discuss see themselves and their work: their self-concept to a very large extent influences the intellectual choices they make, impacting on the content of their thought and the structure of their careers. As Gross keeps reminding us, intellectuals, in making such choices, are in the first place driven by a motivation to develop and defend ideas that resonate with their fundamental self-conceptions. It is this very aspect of Gross's theory that helps us understand the reasons and dynamics underlying position-taking by intellectuals, and the motivational forces behind their choice-making leading to adoption of certain views and actions instead of others. Before moving on to illustrate how this might be so through the example of the Swedish philosopher Vitalis

Norström and the intellectual break he made with the dominant school of thought of his time in his seminal text *Hvad innebär en modern ståndpunkt i filosofien?*, a brief look at the key aspects and features of Norström's biography and that school of thought itself, known in Sweden as Boströmianism, are in order.

Vitalis Norström: From Outdated Idealism to Modern Philosophy of Life

Vitalis Norström (1856–1916) was one of the leading Swedish philosophers of his time and a conservative commentator in cultural debates going on in the country. Raised in privileged conditions in the rural province of Värmland, he, after graduating from high school, relocated to Uppsala in the country's east to attend the prestigious university in the city. There, as he himself put it (Norström 1923, 323), he came "wholly under the influence of Boströmianism," a particular form of idealism that dominated Swedish thought and intellectual life in the second half of the nineteenth century. Norström's doctoral dissertation, *Om undersöfkningen af den gifna verklighetens form* (*On the Investigation of the Given Reality's Form* [1885]), to a notable extent reflects this influence, mediated mostly by the philosopher Boström's primary student and follower Carl Yngve Sahlin (see Åkesson 1954, 73; Nordin 1981, 143; Persson 1994, 90). Following his subsequent appointment as professor of philosophy at the Gothenburg University College (in 1891, with tenure in 1893), Norström soon became something of a poster boy for his young and still small institution (Lindberg and Nilsson 1996, 167). Due to his fluctuating psychological condition, however, he was often forced to take long leaves of absence from his position and interrupt his academic work. In 1898, he nevertheless published his major work *Hvad innebär en modern ståndpunkt i filosofien?* in which he made his public break with the Boströmian school of thought that up until then had been the primary influence on his work. After the turn of the century, Norström's publications gradually came to acquire a more and more popular character. His widely read and publicized texts such as *Ellen Keys tredje rike – en studie öfver radikalismen* (Ellen Key's Third Reich: A Study in Radicalism, 1902) and *Masskultur* (Mass Culture, 1910) strongly shaped the cultural debates of the time in Sweden. In these debates, Norström frequently found himself polemicizing against many of the country's leading cultural figures and intellectuals, among them Ellen Key, Bengt Lidforss, and Hans Larsson. In 1907, he was elected to the Swedish Academy. After his death in 1916, his star nevertheless began to quickly wane. His efforts to attract students to carry on his work had failed, and his successor in Gothenburg, Malte Jacobsson, who was a member of the country's Social Democratic Party, rejected Norström's "modern conservative" outlook, much in keeping with the general social and political climate in the country at the time.

Boströmianism

Christopher Jacob Boström (1797–1866) was professor of practical philosophy at Uppsala University in Sweden (in 1842–1863) whose ideas dominated the philosophical thinking in the country in the nineteenth century. For over fifty years, most of the positions in the country's philosophy departments were held by individuals with a more or less close connection to the kind of philosophy he represented and practiced (Nordin 1981, 11). This philosophy Boström himself termed "rational idealism." The point of departure for his thinking was the postulation that true reality was identical with God and his attributes. These attributes consisted of God's thoughts or ideas, which in themselves were self-conscious rational personalities, with examples of them including both individuals and societies and states. These in turn manifested different degrees of reason and clarity in their power of perception regarding the reality. Consequently, they could be ordered hierarchically according to the degree of rationality and clarity embodied by each. According to Boström, the personalities higher up in the hierarchy encompassed those lower down in it. The highest place in this hierarchy of personal beings was occupied by God, who encompassed all lower-ranking personalities in himself. To illustrate this fundamental postulate of his, Boström often resorted to the natural number sequence. If the number 100 were a self-conscious being, for example, this being would not only be conscious of itself, but also of all the other numbers included in it. The higher personalities, such as God, were thus conscious of the lower personalities and understood them perfectly. However, the lower personalities, such as, for instance, the human consciousness, were themselves conscious of the higher personalities, too, but only in an obscure and imperfect manner.

In Boström's theory of knowledge, everything thus had its own given place in the hierarchy of rational personalities. The location of each personality in this system then determined the degree of clarity of consciousness that was possible for it. Accordingly, human beings, for instance, could not think God's thoughts, being limited by their finite power of perception. For Boström, both time, space, and physical reality were but an illusion rooted in the lower personalities' imperfect powers of perception (Heidegren 2004,

299; Liedman 1991, 114–17; Nordin 1981, 23–25). "Not merely all space, all extension and materia, but also all time, all movement and change is completely excluded from the true and original being" is how Boström himself expressed it (Boström 1883, 481). If, by some miraculous stroke, our power of perception were to suddenly transform and become divine – or at least become capable of rising even a little bit above the phenomenal world – we would discover all these things to actually exist as rational personalities, that is to say, as thoughts of God. The world of senses, in this conception, is merely an illusion that hides the true being of reality. It is hardly surprising, then, that Boström's philosophy came to be accused by Norström of being pre-Kantian in spirit.

Norström's Break with Boströmianism and Critique of Naturalism
As already noted, in Norström's intellectual career the publication of his *Hvad innebär en modern ståndpunkt i filosofien?* marked a clear turning point, a break with this "Boströmian" thinking that hitherto had held him in its sway. In the text, Norström takes a stand against two different philosophical currents at once: on the one hand, the dominating Boströmian philosophy in Sweden and the post-Kantian idealism more generally (Fichte, Schelling, Hegel) and, on the other hand, naturalism. Norström's stated aim in this critical exercise was to outline a third position outside of, but related to, these two, one that he would characterize as "the true modern philosophy" (Norström 1898, XXIX). In stressing this particularly "modern" aspect of his proposed alternative, Norström's point was to challenge naturalism and positivism and their claim to be modernism's standard bearers in his time. In contrast to them, his alternative would "essentially retain the idealistic and rational standpoint" while simultaneously re-casting it within the framework of experience and not, as Boström had done it, outside of it (Norström 1898, XXIX). In other words, Norström's project was to introduce a revamped form of idealism that would better correspond to the expectations set for an idealistic position taken at a time when certain older types of philosophical idealism, such as those formulated by Boström or Hegel, had quite simply lost their credibility. In his *Hvad innebär en modern ståndpunkt i filosofien?* Norström – just as Foucault (1984) much later in his "What Is Enlightenment?," in regard to Kant – thus set about to demarcate his philosophical position in his own time, investigating the standpoints he deemed as possible to take in the "modern" conditions.

In the long introduction he drafted for his text, Norström, the former sympathizer of the position, goes on an at times notably fierce attack against

Boström's rational idealism, which he condemns as pre-Kantian and dogmatic
in its spirit. That a philosophy that in its content was so thorough-goingly pre-
critical had been able to win any adherents at all in the country could, for
him, only be owing to a "psychological mystery" (Norström 1898, XIV). It is,
in other words, with Kant as his weapon that Norström proceeded to disman-
tle the claims and validity of the "Plato of the North," as Boström had come to
be dubbed by his contemporaries. According to Boström, personalities were
absolute, and we could gain knowledge of them through the observation of
the contradictory character of the phenomenal world. That way, he claimed,
we could, with the help of our reason, elevate ourselves above that which was
merely empirical and conditioned and attain knowledge of the eternal concepts (personalities) enthroned beyond the world of phenomena. For Norström, however, knowledge of the absolute was impossible to obtain. True, the
absolute constituted a precondition for knowledge, but it could itself never
become the object of knowledge. This, according to him, was because, fundamentally, "all knowledge takes the form of a judgement" (Norström 1898, IV;
cf. also Norström 1898, 86), and the content of judgements, for its part, always
only drew upon elements that were empirical and contingent in their character and in which no absolute ever made its presence felt. The proclaimed
knowledge of the absolute was about mere "images and phenomena," or, only
rooted in the phenomenal world (Norström 1898, XII). From this then followed, for Norström, that we could not attain any richer knowledge of concepts (personalities) by moving beyond that which was empirical. Knowledge,
he declared, was obtained by intuition (*anschauung*), not through abstract
thinking. Similarly to Kant, concepts without percepts were for him empty.
Mere conceptual analysis could never result in arrival at substantial meta-
physical truths; the only kind of knowledge possible for human beings was
that of "the thing itself, the perceivable, in the last instance always concrete
and individual object" (Norström 1898, VIII). For this reason, we cannot, as
Boström postulated, escape from the phenomenal world; reason and concepts always refer us back to an empirical and historical context, to that which
is "the given" (Norström 1898, IX).

Post-Kantian idealism à la Fichte, Schelling, and Hegel, could, according to
Norström (1898, XVII), be criticized in this connection for having developed
Kantian thought in a "fantastical direction." Adopting empty abstractions
that never were given concrete historical grounding as the starting point for
their philosophizing, the thinkers in this line of enquiry had ended up con-
travening the critical principles that Kant had laid out. They ascribed agency

to abstract ideas and concepts without understanding that ideas could only be borne by concrete human (or divine) subjects (Norström 1898, XX). Thus, what was common to both Boströmianism and post-Kantian idealism was their disloyalty to Kant's critique of knowledge, which they had manifested by departing outside the realm of sensory experience, that which is immediately given in our perception. In both cases, the result was an abstract philosophy, one that lacked real content grounded in experience. According to Norström, such philosophy, one that left behind the realm of experience, could only end up losing itself in "the hocus-pocus of construction," or a type of philosophy that, more or less, engaged in mere postulation of what was required to prove statements (Norström 1898, XX).

The second main target of Norström's critique was naturalism. Just as idealism, so also naturalism had showed itself deficient in its analysis of personal experience. The mistake was in both cases the same: the point of departure was not in the concrete, given experience, but in abstractions made out of experience (Norström 1998, XXI; Persson 1994, 145). In fact, the very notion of experience in naturalism was severely constricted, indeed mutilated: limiting experience to concern only that which was sensuous in nature meant that "rational experiences," as Norström called them, consisting of our religious and ethical experiences, were excluded and even precluded. Experience, according to Norström, had to be more broadly conceived in terms of its (possible) content, and that meant including in it not only sensory experiences, but also religious and ethical ones. Such "rational experiences" deserved to be considered as a fact and could under no circumstances be discounted or misrepresented (Norström 1898, XXXIV). Nor were they, it needed to be stressed, entirely subjective in nature, but afforded actual insight into, or a glimpse of, the rational developments unfolding in human history. In religious experiences and the human feeling for solidarity, moreover, there was to be found undeniable evidence that cultural development was steered by divine will, and that this development was towards the ultimate realization of God's kingdom (Norström 1898, 36). The validity of such experiences could, however, not be established empirically or through deductive reasoning, for the kind of knowledge they conveyed was only attainable in the form of feeling and symbols. Nevertheless, Norström maintained, this fact did not exclude the possibility that they could all the same allow an insight into the true being of reality, or, reality as it was in and of its own nature.

Although relying on Kant to criticize both Boström and German idealism, Norström, to be sure, was not uncritical in his relation to the former,

either. Contrary to Kant, he refused to draw a sharp, unbridgeable distinction
between theoretical and practical reason, preferring rather to base the former in the latter. Theoretical reason, according to him, possessed no autonomy of its own, remaining dependent on what Norström termed "rational
experiences": it, as our capacity for knowledge, was rooted in our will and
feeling, in our practical reason. The concepts formed through theoretical
understanding were, in themselves, no more than empty abstractions that in
reality never escaped their determination in the last instance by experiences
of will and feeling. What this meant is that practical reason was always primary in relation to theoretical reason, which then emerged as an effect of will
and feeling.

In his 1899 text "Hvad är sanning?" ("What Is Truth?," originally intended
as a companion piece to *Hvad innebär en modern ståndpunkt i filosofien?*), Norström further elaborated on his thesis regarding the dependence of all our
knowledge on will. In it, Norström introduces his view on science and truth as
ultimately instrumental and pragmatic in nature. Natural science, he maintained, did not present truthful depictions of reality, but offered, in the first
place, a practical tool with which to pursue certain cultural interests, such as
the curing of diseases or the building of bridges. Insofar as it only occupies
itself with what ultimately amounts to no more than fiction, furthermore, we
are free to relate to its descriptions of reality as we wish without its having to
negatively impact our relationship to religion. Thereby, "our mind is freed
from the desiccating influence that the mechanical worldview has on the
fountainhead of our very life. It is the worst bane under which our modern
culture groans that it [mechanical worldview] sees imagination and lies in
everything that does not conform to the key axiom of naturalism by refusing
to be just a cogwheel in nature's great, cold, and dead machinery" (Norström
1905a, 21).

Theoretical reason, in other words, disallowed certain thought-combina-
tions as self-contradictory, but beyond that we were in principle free to assume
whichever attitude we wished towards both natural sciences and religion and
ethics.

Understanding and Explaining Norström's Intellectual Choices
What the sociology of philosophy seeks to do is find explanations for why
thinkers within the field of philosophy adopt certain theoretical standpoints
rather than others. The question therefore poses itself as to whether it might
be possible to find a sociological or social-psychological explanation for the

above-described intellectual choices that the Swedish thinker Vitalis Norström made in the course of his philosophical career. My own suggestion is to turn to Gross's theory of intellectual self-concept as a promising avenue of pursuit in this regard, since, as it seems to me, it is possible to better comprehend and render intelligible the different positions and viewpoints he promulgated and embraced in his *Hvad innebär en modern ståndpunkt i filosofien?* if we take as our point of departure his self-understanding of himself as the philosopher of the personal and rational life. Before taking a closer look at how Gross's theory might be applicable to Norström's thinking and career, however, I will first consider possible alternative explanations of Bourdieuian and Collinsian type to Norström's intellectual choices, to show what can be achieved with them but why they nevertheless can but ultimately fall short of the task.

As Collins has noted, one powerful and oft-used way to garner attention around oneself in the field of philosophy is to seek third positions, proceeding from "a plague on both your houses" type of argumentation (Collins 2000, 81). For him, philosophical activity in the main consists not so much of problem solving as it does of the discovery of "exploitable lines of opposition" (Collins 2000, 6). When, in other words, a philosopher rises up to proclaim "A" (e.g., Boström and his rational idealism above), with another one then objecting with "Not A" (positivism, naturalism), there is thus always the possibility to assert "Neither A nor Not A, but B" (Norström's "modern standpoint in philosophy"). An analysis departing from Collins's theory would thus, in our present case, focus on how Norström seeks a niche for himself in the field of philosophy where his own ideas could negate the central ones dominating in the area. To apply such a schematic and a priori view on Norström's development would, however, in my opinion do violence to the fundamental biographical facts of the case. In an 1899 letter to the theologian Samuel Fries, for instance, Norström wrote that, all its shortcomings notwithstanding, his *Hvad innebär en modern ståndpunkt i filosofien?* had a distinct merit: "it is a 'document humain' a record in the medium of abstract thought of hard-won personal development" (Norström 1923, 108). In another letter, to his colleague Erik Olof Burman in 1895, Norström speaks of his own "history of emancipation" from transcendental philosophy (for him, German idealism) that had been "dwelling on me like a nightmare, giving me unpleasant dreams" (Norström 1923, 42). Several years later, in yet another letter, he spoke of the hard blow that it was for him to discover that the rationality of existence was something that could not be proven, only believed in and hoped for (Norström 1923,

278). In other words, it could hardly be a case here of strategically orienting oneself towards seizing and occupying new positions in the philosophical field (cf. Heidegren 2004, 454, 467; Persson 1994, 140). Instead, what we are clearly described is an utterly conscious and deliberate personal struggle.

Another kind of explanation for the standpoints put forth in *Hvad innebär en modern ståndpunkt i filosofien?*, one that proceeds from a Bourdieuian perspective, would in one respect look largely similar. Even now would one be interested in analysing how Norström sought to create a name for himself by strategically navigating forward in the field of philosophy as it appeared to him in the late nineteenth-century Swedish context, Norström's own self-understanding of himself would have no place in such an examination. A Bourdieuian-influenced researcher would, however – just has Bourdieu does in his *Political Ontology* – attempt to indirectly couple Norström's philosophical position-taking to political standpoints outside the field. By virtue of that characteristic alone, this angle of approach to Norström's intellectual life is already far more interesting to consider than any attempt to sketch Norström's path as one of a mere careerist.

It is not impossible, as Persson (1994, 393) has suggested, to find Norström's philosophy as something emblematic of the long drawn-out death throes of the old society. Norström's attempt to rejuvenate idealism in his *Hvad innebär en modern ståndpunkt i filosofien?* could, accordingly, be interpreted as an ideological vindication of a social system having come under political pressure – a system that had previously been taken for granted but which now had suddenly been forced to defend itself. There is quite much that speaks in favour of this understanding. There was a conservative and idealistic-religious worldview that, in nineteenth-century Sweden, had come to exert a great influence on the country's cultural and social life. It not only provided the groundwork on which intellectual life and science were built in the society, but also served as a foundation for many people's way of life (Persson 1994, 114). To express it in Bourdieu's terms, we might summarize it as having become a constituent element of the upper classes' class habitus in the country. In his article "Hvad är sanning?," Norström claimed that one notable property of his instrumentalist view of science was that it left the idealistic worldview intact: "Without concern for the formulas of science, stories and sagas can still weave their gilded motif into the fabric of life and the blue flower of Romanticism can continue to flourish in the shadow of the spruce that whispers about love of home, the native country, and the church" (Norström 1905a, 28). A sociologist of philosophy following in Bourdieu's footsteps would seek to show that

Norström's embracement of an instrumentalist view of science had its correspondence in his embracement of an idealistic-conservative worldview in the field of politics. The two positions, in other words, were related to each other as homologous.

Indeed, the particular version of idealism that Norström put forth was received with much enthusiasm by those representing the more conservative circles in the society. Norström's philosophy was seen as having overcome naturalism and, thereby, deprived the forces of the political left of their foremost weapon. In this connection it is, however, important to distinguish between ideological function and motive (cf. Persson 1994, 282). The reception of Norström's *Hvad innebär en modern ståndpunkt i filosofien?* and other writings showed his work to have had clear political implications. If, however, we want to understand the fundamental motives guiding Norström's thinking, it would be misleading to start out from the general observation that Norström overall was politically conservative. The danger with this kind of sociology-of-knowledge explanations is that the object of the analysis quickly disappears from the picture: complex and intricate philosophical thought processes and lines of reasoning easily become re-interpreted as strategies claimed to be geared toward vindicating a certain social order. Norström's philosophy will, consequently, be reduced to an instinctive, though ultimately futile, attempt to rescue as much as possible of the pre-modern qualities of Sweden. It was in a similar way that Bourdieu himself regarded Heidegger and his philosophy. According to Bourdieu, Heidegger was less the subject than the object in relation to his habitus, and, without realizing it himself, was thus more or less condemned to serve as a medium for the socio-political forces of his time to express themselves through his work (Bourdieu 1991, 105; Lundberg 2014).

An analysis along these lines, however, misses that which is unique and specific to Norström. To paraphrase Sartre's famous riposte of Valéry (Sartre 1960, 80), Norström was a politically conservative philosopher, no doubt about it, but not every politically conservative philosopher was a Norström. There was also something about Norström that made him (more or less) unique as a philosophical thinker in Sweden in his time, something that resists neat categorization in terms as general and universal as "politically conservative philosopher" and "upper-class habitus." Behind the impulses of his thought and thinking lay always his deep existential engagement with personal life. At its core, his philosophy was all about creating a space for that kind of life in the climate of ideas in which he worked.

Norström's self-concept and his philosophical position-taking in the "Hvad innebär en modern ståndpunkt i filosofien?"

Norström's intellectual choices in his *Hvad innebär en modern ståndpunkt i filosofien?* were based first and foremost on his self-understanding of himself as a champion of the personal and rational life vis-à-vis the soulless and irrational elements of the existence. As he explained to his friend Ernst Liljedahl in a personal letter, his struggle was one aimed at personal liberation, at "breaking out of the confines of life-suffocating theories" (Liljedahl 1917, I: 329). This struggle, I maintain, is of critical importance for understanding and explaining the theoretical choices Norström made in this key work of his. Its significance in this regard, as I will try to make clear below, is made evident by his correspondence dating from the time when he worked on his manuscript for the *Hvad innebär en modern ståndpunkt i filosofien?* and shortly thereafter. In his letters from this period, Norström, among other things, describes the mystical experiences that to a large extent came to form the cornerstone of his thinking and self-concept. According to the theory of intellectual self-concept, narratives such as these serve the purpose of re-organizing the image intellectuals have of themselves and their work and of integrating the two. From the narratives Norström put forth in his letters, a picture of him emerges that one also finds, albeit on another plane, coming to expression in his *Hvad innebär en modern ståndpunkt i filosofien?*

In his correspondence with his colleague Erik Olof Burman, Norström addresses the personal motives lying behind his break with Boströmianism. In a letter from December 1895, he, for instance, writes of his feelings of relief after having succeeded in leaving this current of thinking behind and moving on:

> I feel myself immensely happy about having been able to free myself from the yoke of Boströmianism. I have only more and more come to realize how crude its standpoint is as concerns its pretence to scientific credibility, and how it allows for only scant or no room for the sense of nature and art, for the mystery of feeling and for full and wholly religious life. In truth: there is so much shallowness and superficiality! And unspirituality! (Norström 1923, 60)

In another letter to Burman, from one month later, Norström turned towards Burman's own "idealistic evolutionism," criticizing it on the grounds that it implied an "abstract-impersonal attitude in which the concept has expelled the spirit" and thereby left no room for "religious experience" (Norström 1923, 65–66). A still later (1899) letter to the same addressee finds Norström proclaiming himself to be against all teachings that "do away with the sense of individualism and personality by presenting man to be, as it were, not much more than a mechanical or a logical cog in a soulless mechanism." In Norström's view, Swedish philosophy had not done enough to settle its relation to the kind of "impersonal feelings and sentiments" that threatened to suffocate any incipient or budding "personal life," such as "the feeling of the universality of the nature-mechanism, the dynamistic or pantheistic Nature-feeling, the feeling of an all-embracing social mechanism, of history as a logical process, etc." (Norström 1923, 106).

As becomes evident from this quote, Norström in this letter turned his critical focus on both naturalistic and idealistic standpoints, the very same way he does in his *Hvad innebär en modern ståndpunkt i filosofien?* What the two different kinds of philosophy shared in common was rejection of the meaning of the free and personal life. Neither idealism nor naturalism left any room for rational experiences gained through the "mystery of feeling" or "religious life." German idealism, in Norström's view, had failed to anchor rational historical development in "any real cause, leaving it instead freely floating in a space of abstraction without a concrete, factual, and historical foundation" (Norström 1898, XIX). Everything "concrete and individual" could thereby but appear as no more than "secondary (a result, an effect, a consequence)" in relation to the abstract concepts put forth by the German idealists, such as Hegel's World Spirit (Norström 1898, XIX). An understanding of history as something driven by an impersonal principle, "a logical process," thus excluded the possibility of a free and personal life in the exact same way this happened in naturalism. Indeed, a conception of history along these lines, according to Norström, meant that "the spirit [was] once again surreptitiously reduced to nature" (Norström 1923, 233).

Norström's critical attitude towards the impersonal and the abstract, however, manifested itself in also other positions he adopted in *Hvad innebär en modern ståndpunkt i filosofien?* In the work, he, among other things, made the objection that Boström's concept of God was an empty abstraction that had nothing to do with the God of Abraham, Isaac and Jacob, the God of the Bible and the Christian Faith. Boström's God, according to Norström, was "a mere hypostatized abstraction, a mere thought-object, having in a most dubious manner been left floating free of any historical-empirical moorings" (Norström 1898, IX). Such an abstract and impersonal notion of God was something Norström was unable to accept. At the same time, however, he was also unable to embrace a rigid and dogmatic Christianity that did not place personal life at its centre. "The inner measure of Christianity is its value for nurturing and nourishing life," he summed up his position; its truth claim quite simply lay in its ability to foster personal life (Norström 1905b, 114).

Norström's advocacy of the personal life, I argue, to a large extent derived from his own personal experiences. It was in these that his intellectual self-concept in the last instance had its origins. Norström's life was studded with mental crises, but also with religious experiences. In an 1898 letter to his friend Karl Warburg, Norström describes the impact that two separate incidents involving the latter had on him as revelations of a mystical kind:

> These experiences have given me certainty that there is a rational world-coherence, that there is a God, an infinite life-content and life perspective for the spirit. My apperception of all this, to be sure, has unfolded entirely through the medium of feeling and not at all of observation or sensory experience, but this feeling experience has been substantial enough to support my life. (Norström 1923, 102)

These experiences were in line with what the theory of knowledge Norström presented in his *Hvad innebär en modern ståndpunkt i filosofien?* states. The apperception he describes did not result in acquired new knowledge in any ordinary sense, but in a feeling of assurance as to the rational nature of reality.[5] In a letter to Allen Vannérus from 1900, moreover, Norström wrote that "the secret to my philosophy is that it is a manifestation of how deeply I am affected by life. Its sources are in lived experiences" (Norström 1923, 118). It was these experiences, then, that according to Norström himself had given rise to his philosophy. Essentially, the latter could therefore only be refuted by his own further life experiences and not by other thinkers' arguments. That, moreover, would only be able to happen if, due to extraneous circumstances, he were forced to give up his faith in personal reason and rationality in his-

---

5 In an autobiographical sketch from 1912, Norström (1923, 323) writes about these experiences of his as follows: "From these crises I have already three times been rescued through temporally and spatially distinct experiences of 'raptus in coelom', which I nevertheless hold as entirely real and as absolutely necessary for the maintenance of spiritual health and strength. But they all have fallen within the domain of *feeling*. No visions! An experience of the rationality of the world's foundations." In another letter, to Oscar Lindberg in 1894, he speaks of how "on two unforgettable occasions in my life" he had felt a 'rush of God's power and mercy' when finding himself in a deep crisis (Liljedahl 1917, vol. I, 174). While it is impossible to establish the exact dates of these experiences, the third occasion he speaks of must have been sometime between 1898 and 1912.

tory. Thus far, he had nevertheless never been driven to despair, although he had "more than once felt the wings of the black bird flap" (Norström 1923, 119).

Further testimony about such experiences of Norström's can be found in yet another letter he wrote to Burman, from 1898. In earlier correspondence, Burman had criticized *Hvad innebär en modern ståndpunkt i filosofien?* on the grounds that it built on elements of mysticism, which he for his part firmly rejected. In his reply, Norström described mysticism as something that ran counter to his very nature, but which nevertheless had "its roots in my personal experiences. ... Compared to the holy that has befallen me, is everything else not darkness, is everything else not folly? From that I want to live – and learn" (Norström 1923, 99). In another personal letter, to Oscar Ljungström in December 1907, Norström's describes his sense of calling in this regard in even greater detail. In response to Ljungström's attempt to interest Norström in theosophy, in vogue in the country at the time, he stated that he was afraid of veering off the staked-out path. "Once, when caught in a burning struggle and deep despair, a spirit came over me – all on its own from the inside. It was many years ago, but from that experience I still today draw my nourishment. It is for me a wellspring from which to draw, one that gives me what I need in matters of faith and hope. From it flows also the work I do, which must follow a certain definite course by which I stand [or] fall. I am firmly fixed on this path of mine" (Liljedahl 1917, vol. II, 34).

The mystical experiences Norström had had, in other words, provided the foundation from which both his life and his intellectual choices were then determinedly built. Based on them, as becomes clear from his letters to his colleagues and friends, Norström developed a self-concept, both for himself as well as for others, as an opponent equally of the "mechanical" (naturalism) and the "abstract" (idealism), and as a defender and champion of the personal and rational life. It was this self-concept that then came to illuminate his "staked-out path," and it was it that also led him to adopt a certain specific position within the field of philosophy as a consequence.

The Infrastructure of Intellectual Life

To understand the process by which Norström came to adopt and occupy his position within the field of philosophy in Sweden, it is, however, also necessary to include in the examination an analysis on macro and meso levels. In line with the contemporary sociology of ideas (Camic and Gross 2001; Gross 2011), my argument is that factors on these levels in the first place had an indirect influence on Norström's thinking and thought, through changes they brought in the material conditions of intellectual activity. These changed conditions in Norström's case consisted first and foremost of the establishment of a new professorial chair at the Gothenburg University College (today the University of Gothenburg) in the country's second-largest city. Upon being appointed to this position (Professor of Philosophy) in 1891, Norström left Uppsala to take residence in Gothenburg. As several commentators have noted, this move, from the tradition-bound provincial city of Uppsala to the young, modern, and expansive Gothenburg, probably contributed much to Norström's subsequent break with Boströmianism (Åkesson 1954, 74–75; Nordin 1981, 148; Persson 1994, 184). In Heidegren's (2004, 454) estimation, Norström most likely would not have been able to follow through with this project of his had he stayed on in the closed environment that Uppsala at the time represented: the pressure from tradition and those around him would most certainly been too much for him to overcome. Indeed, as Heidegren has noted, very much in line with Nordic commentators on Boströmianism in Norström's own time, to be situated in a relatively isolated small-town academic environment like Uppsala was even a precondition for a philosophical school like Boströmianism to take root, engage, and flourish.

The decision to establish the Gothenburg University College had been made by the city's municipal council in November 1887. To set up new colleges and universities was not a unique phenomenon in the country at the time, but conformed to the more general trend of expanding higher education in late nineteenth-century Europe standing in need of more and better trained workers for its industrializing and modernizing sectors (Lindberg and Nilsson 1996, 31). Seven professorial chairs were created for the Gothenburg University College, with one of them being for philosophy. Adding to the already existing philosophy professorships in the country, in Lund and Uppsala, this was the fifth chair to be set up in the field in Sweden. Through a political decision on the meso level, the infrastructure for intellectual life was thus considerably expanded in the country. The new professorship in Gothenburg, to be sure, could not boast an academic status comparable to that of the state professorships in Lund and Uppsala, but it nevertheless implied an opening up of a possibility for developing a new position in the field. As a necessary social condition for abstract and advanced thinking, as opposed to pure practical thinking, is, as Bourdieu (2000) has pointed out, the ability of intellectuals to access *skhole*, or time that one can devote to intellectual rather than pure physical labour, to the extent that through his professorial appointment Norström could then do just that, he could, as he himself put it in a letter to his friend Oscar Lindberg, thus now freely dedicate himself with all his powers and energies to his "beloved science" and to developing his intellectual positions without having to worry about his finances (Liljedahl 1917, vol. I, 172).

In other words, changes in the meso level were necessary for Norström to be able to proceed to develop a new and sufficiently original intellectual standpoint in his national context. These changes had two primary consequences: on the one hand, through them Norström gained access to *skhole*, and, on the other hand, they made it possible for him to leave the closed environment he found himself caught up in in Uppsala. Both of these consequences, in turn, then had the enabling effect of making it possible for him to more freely give expression to, and act upon, his intellectual self-concept.

Strategic Conditioning or Choice Based on Intellectual Self-Concept?

As becomes clear from above, the way Gross himself sees his theory is that it complements the view of theoretical choices as being exclusively conditioned by strategic considerations. Nevertheless, it remains ultimately unclear how Gross understands the way the two explanatory types, one focussing on strategic choice and the other choice based on one's intellectual self-concept, relate to each other (cf. Heidegren and Lundberg 2010, 16). He never provides a clear account of this, merely noting that the two different action types involved can often co-exist in influencing the course of a philosopher's career.[6] As he himself puts it, "the actions thinkers undertake to remain true to their self-concepts unfold alongside and in conjunction with other,

---

6 According to the theory of intellectual self-concept, academics are more prone to act strategically early on in their careers, before succeeding to establish a position for themselves within the academia; it is only after the latter that questions of self-concept and identity become more important to them than strategically navigating the field. The validity of this thesis is, however, difficult to verify in the case of Norström, for which reason I have omitted any closer examination of this aspect of Gross' theory (for a discussion of methodological challenges in the study of motives behind intellectual choices, see Baert [2012, 307–308]). Applied to Norström's case, the theory of intellectual self-concept would, however, likely propose that Norström was a fairly loyal Boströmian until securing a permanent position for himself, after which he could allow his own self-concept to fully come to the fore and start steering his thinking and actions. What is clear at any rate is that Norström's public break with Boströmianism occurred only after his appointment to a permanent professorship in May 1893. As appears from above, however, my own interpretation is that this departure from Boströmianism came first and foremost as a result of Norström's leaving behind the constricted environment of Uppsala, which for him entailed an increased ability to freely express his self-concept. This does nevertheless not mean that Norström thereby ceased to be motivated by intellectual vanity and/or ambition in his actions (see, e.g., his August 1909 letter to Oscar Lindberg, cited in Liljedahl 1917, vol. II, 140). Nonetheless, there is no direct evidence anywhere in his texts, or in those by others, that this would in any way have influenced the cognitive content of his philosophy.

more strategic action processes" (Gross 2008, 264). The problem with this conception, however, is that it presents us with two different types of explanation that pull in opposite directions. Strategic action is (unconsciously) oriented to maximizing one's possession of scarce resources, such as one's colleagues' attention or prominent positions. In field theorizing (such as by Collins and Bourdieu) it is thus the field itself that is the ultimate subject and explanatory principle of philosophy. In actions based on one's (conscious) self-concept, developed or acquired to a large degree outside of the field, the orientation is, instead, toward maintenance or preservation of actors' self-concepts. To a certain extent, then, where actors make choices to remain true to their self-concepts, explaining their resulting actions as strategically oriented will be misleading. An intellectual self-identity sets limits to what theoretical choices are possible for one to make, which in turn limits one's ability to compete in the field. Norström, for instance, could most likely never have embraced a naturalistic standpoint, even if this would have brought him fame, reputation, and influence. Indeed, Gross agrees that not all choices are open to a philosopher to make, and that the two different kinds of explanation can stand even in a conflictual relation to each other. As he himself describes the more extreme consequences of their ultimate incompatibility, "[t]he psychic costs of a wholly instrumental orientation in which one agrees to abandon or change any or all of identity and intellectual commitments as may be required by the logic of the field would be too much to bear" (Gross 2008, 310; cf. 238).

This view contrasts starkly with, for example, Collins's understanding of philosophical activity. For Collins, the logic of that activity is wholly subject to the logic of the field, for instance through the law of small numbers obeyed by intellectual dynamics (Collins 2008, 81–82). Collins's philosophers strive to combine cultural capital in as novel or even revolutionary ways as possible, so as to be able to attract attention to themselves and their work. In doing so, there is nothing to limit the kind of choices available to them to promote their goals; the logic of the field dominates unchallenged. It is on that very account that it remains unclear to what extent the theory of intellectual self-concept could be said to complement Bourdieu's and Collins's type theorizing by taking "a broadened conception of identity into account" (Gross 2008, 239). In fact, the two types of explanation seem rather to contradict than complement each other: if Gross is right in his claims, his theory would seem to me to constitute something more like a refutation of Collins's and Bourdieu's arguments than their necessary counterpart.

Concluding Discussion

The task of the sociology of philosophy ought not be to first construct a more or less a priori theoretical framework for analysis and then sort out empirical facts in accordance with it. In a sociological study of philosophers and their work, it is important that individual biographies be fully taken into account and allowed to influence the analysis without glossing over their complexity (cf. Gross 2008, 15). In Norström's case, as seen above, the choice of one's theoretical standpoints, such as this philosopher's public break with Boströmianism, hardly allows itself to be explicated in terms of either strategic action within the field of philosophy or un-reflected ideological defence of a pre-modern society. The problem marring both Bourdieu's and Collins's work in this area (Bourdieu 1991; Collins 2000) is that the analyses put forth by the two are not detailed enough, moving as they do exclusively on macro and meso levels. Even where Collins (2000, 53) himself may proclaim that it is "the flow of micro-situations that is the topic of [his] story," his book contains no analyses of, or even references to, diaries, conferences, letters, and other historical material of relevance for micro-level investigation. Neither does one find in Bourdieu's key work on the topic (1991) any actual analyses of micro-level data. Yet, when starting from the micro level, for instance through a study of personal letters and other correspondence, much of that which is taken for granted in more abstract theorizing quickly becomes problematized. This seems evident enough to allow for, even warrant, the formulation of the following general claim: the more in depth one examines any given case, the more obvious it becomes how important questions of self-concept and identity are for understanding theory choices of intellectuals. The accuracy and validity of this statement can, however, only be confirmed by further empirical studies that take the theory of intellectual self-concept as their starting point.

In this article, I have argued that the content of the Swedish philosopher Vitalis Norström's "modern standpoint in philosophy" can be explained through his engagement and advocacy on behalf of the possibilities for a genuinely personal life, which involvement, for its part, to a notably high degree stemmed from, and built on, his mystical experiences. Norström's intellectual self-concept led him to rise against both philosophers constructing idealistic systems and thinkers adhering to naturalism and positivism, on grounds that none of these philosophical schools left any room for "rational experiences" of individuals. The micro level is, however, not the only analytical level on which the theory of intellectual self-concept operates; as shown above, there

are also important meso and macro-level factors shaping the material precon-
ditions for philosophical thought that need to be accounted for. As concerns
Norström and his philosophical position-taking in his key work *Hvad innebär
en modern ståndpunkt i filosofien?*, one can distinguish factors impinging upon
the development of his philosophical thinking on all three of these levels.
These can be presented in a summary format as follows:

- Macro level: Modernization processes, expansion of the educational
  system in Europe.
- Meso level: Establishment of a new professorial chair at the Gothenburg
  University College in 1891.
- Micro level: Norström's self-understanding of himself as a defender of
  the personal and rational life.

As argued above, Norström's "modern standpoint" would very likely not
have been possible to develop and pronounce without the establishment of
the new professorial chair in Gothenburg and Norström's accession to the
position. Two circumstances in particular contributed to the critical change
in Norström's working conditions that his move to Gothenburg entailed:
first, leaving behind the restricted intellectual atmosphere of Uppsala enabled him to develop the same kind of outsider's perspective on Boströmianism that also other contemporary commentators on it had, and, second, the
professorship that was offered him in Gothenburg provided him with access
to *skhole*. These changes on the meso level were themselves linked to other,
more large-scale societal changes unfolding in Europe at the time, developments brought by processes of modernization. In line with the postulates of
the new sociology of ideas, the influence that these macro and meso-level
changes had on the content of Norström's intellectual work were, however,
first and foremost only indirect in nature. Nevertheless, it is also important
to keep in mind that Norström formulated his intellectual position in such
a way as to at the same time allow him to respond to the demand heard in
his time for a "modern standpoint" in philosophy. The collapse of idealistic philosophical systems had forced him to work out a new position based
on the question of the role of philosophy in the new, still evolving society
whose outlines were only beginning to become clear. In this way, social and
societal (macro) factors in the form of modernization processes constituted
the background against which Norström's renewed philosophical idealism
then came to take shape. Yet, even here the question is clearly more about

indirect rather than direct impact that such factors may have had on him, his thinking, and his work.

The observation I have put forth that understanding Norström's personal background is important for understanding his thinking is hardly pioneering even in the case of this particular thinker. The same has been pointed out by many other historians of ideas and philosophy, including several referred to in this article. What is new about it in the present context is that it results from an systematically effort to link Norström's self-understanding and self-concept to his intellectual position-taking in his main work where he lays out the elements of what was to constitute one of his lasting contributions to Swedish philosophy. The connection between the two is of particular interest to ongoing debates over how to understand and explain individuals' intellectual choices from a sociological perspective. In this regard, the analysis presented above supports Gross's view that, in a sociological examination of philosophical activity, one should not disregard philosophers' own self-understandings of themselves, their self-concepts. Nevertheless, there is, as already noted, also reason to criticize the theory of intellectual self-concept, for not having sufficiently clarified how strategic action and actions undertaken to remain true to one's self-concept in fact relate to each other as explanatory principles and analytical concepts.

One can, furthermore, pose the question of whether adopting the theory of intellectual self-concept might not in the end mean abandoning the project of the sociology of knowledge in favour of a more restricted undertaking aimed at a mere psychological understanding of philosophers and their intellectual identity. Self-concept – is that not a concept of psychology? No, not only, would Gross's own answer go; identity is created in social contexts, such as through one's religious affiliation, membership in associations and organizations, family and kinship relations, education and academic affiliation, political party membership, and so on (Gross 2008, 15–16). Many of the identities adopted by intellectuals are, furthermore, pre-determined: they, like "left-leaning sociologist," "liberal economist," and the like, constitute culturally specific taxonomies, fixed in advance, that supply intellectuals with the possible identities among which to then choose. Vitalis Norström in Sweden interpreted his mystical experiences from a religious point of view. It would have, however, also been possible, even if not for Norström personally, to give those experiences a strictly naturalistic reading. For Norström, it was his socialization and educational history that had pre-disposed him towards a certain (religious, instead of naturalistic) interpretive frame, which then made his experiences to become for him a call to fight theories that "aspire to narrow down, limit, and impoverish life" (Norström 1905, 347). Given another kind of history of socialization and a different view of the world, it is highly conceivable that Norström would have ended up with another kind of self-concept and other theory choices. The culturally specific notions of identity that nineteenth-century Sweden with its dominant religious-idealistic worldview could offer to young intellectuals looked very different from those available in the country's society today. Self-concepts are, accordingly, always thoroughly and irreducibly social as a phenomenon. Therefore, the study of intellectual self-concepts, too, must always remain sociological and social-psychological as a project.

References

Åkesson, E. 1954. *Punkter på ljuslinjen. Idéhistoriska bidrag.* Lund: Gleerups.

Baert, P. 2012. "Positioning Theory and Intellectual Interventions." *Journal for the Theory of Social Behaviour* 42: 304–24.

Boström, C.J. [1859] 1883. *C.J. Boström och hans philosophi.* Skrifter av Christopher Jacob Boström utgifvna av Edfeldt, Hans, Upsala.

Bourdieu, Pierre. 1991. *The Political Ontology of Martin Heidegger.* Cambridge, UK: Polity Press.

———. 2000. *Pascalian Meditations.* Cambridge, UK: Polity Press.

Bryant, J.M. 2011. "New Directions and Perennial Challenges in the Sociology of Philosophy: Theoretical and Methodological Notes on Neil Gross's *Richard Rorty*." *Transactions of Charles S. Peirce Society: A Quarterly Journal in American Philosophy* 47: 32–27.

Camic, Charles, and Neil Gross. 2001. "The New Sociology of Ideas." In *The Blackwell Companion to Sociology*, edited by J.R. Blau, 236–49. Oxford: Blackwell.

Collins, Randall. 2000. *The Sociology of Philosophies: A Global Theory of Intellectual Change.* Cambridge, MA: Belknap Press.

Foucault, Michel. 1984. "What is Enlightenment?" In *The Foucault Reader*, edited by P. Rainbow, 32–50. New York: Pantheon.

Gross, Neil. 2008. *Richard Rorty: The Making of an American Philosopher.* Chicago and London: University of Chicago Press.

———. 2011. "Replies." *Transactions of Charles S Peirce Society: A Quarterly Journal in American Philosophy* 47: 46–61.

Gross, Neil, and Crystal Fleming. 2011. "Academic Conferences and the Making of Philosophical Knowledge." In *Social Knowledge in the Making*, edited by C. Camic, N. Gross, and M. Lamont, 151–79. Chicago and London: University of Chicago Press.

Heidegren, C.-G. 2004. *Det moderna genombrottet i nordisk universitetsfilosofi 1860–1915.* Göteborg: Daidalos.

Heidegren, C.-G., and Henrik Lundberg. 2010. "Towards a Sociology of Philosophy." *Acta Sociologica* 53: 3–18.

Kusch, Martin. 1995. *Psychologism: A Case Study in the Sociology of Philosophical Knowledge.* London: Routledge.

Liedman, S.-E. 1991. *Att förändra världen men med måtta. Det svenska 1800-talet speglat i C.A. Agardhs och C.J. Boströms liv och verk* Stockholm: Arbetarkultur.

Liljedahl, E. 1917–1918. *Vitalis Norström. Hans liv och verk I–II.* Stockholm: Svenska kyrkans diakonistyrelses bokförlag.

Lindberg, B., and I. Nilsson. 1996. *Göteborgs universitets historia. På högskolans tid.* Göteborg: Rektorsämbetet Göteborgs universitet.

Lundberg, Henrik. 2014. "Philosophical Thought and its Existential Basis: The Sociologies of Philosophy of Randall Collins and Pierre Bourdieu." *Transcultural Studies* 10: 119–46.

Nordin, S. 1981. *Den Boströmska skolan och den svenska idealismens fall.* Lund: Doxa.

Norström, Vitalis. 1898. *Hvad innebär en modern ståndpunkt i filosofien?* Göteborgs Högskolas Årsskrifter IV:1. Göteborg: Göteborgs Högskola.

———. [1902] 1905. "Ellen Keys tredje rike. En studie öfver radikalismen." In *Tankelinier,* 158–298. Stockholm: Hierta.

———. 1905a. "Hvad är sanning?" In *Tankelinier,* 2–36. Stockholm: Hierta.

———. 1905b. "Förnuftskraf." In *Tankelinier,* 64–157. Stockholm: Hierta.

———. 1905c. "Den religiösa kunskapen." In *Tankelinier,* 299–411. Stockholm: Hierta.

———. 1910. *Masskultur.* Stockholm: Hierta.

Norström, V. 1923. *Brev 1889–1916 i urval utgivna av Elof Åkesson.* Stockholm: Fritzes.

Persson, M. 1994. *Förnuftskampen. Vitalis Norström och idealismens kris.* Stehag: Brutus Östlings bokförlag Symposion.

Sartre, Jean Paul. 1960. *Questions de méthode* Paris: Gallimard.

Political *Personas* and the Fundaments of Democratic Society

On the Ethical Ontology of María Zambrano

Karolina Enquist Källgren

Abstract

This study analyses the political thinking of the Spanish philosopher María Zambrano (1904–1991). By focusing on the notions *persona* and *individuo* it argues that Zambrano's entire thought must be interpreted in the light of the ethical ontology present in her political writings. The study contextualizes Zambrano's political writings and shows that the circumstances of Zambrano's exile can explain why she opted for a discussion on politics that emphasizes personal responsibility rather than the political organization of society. The study further shows that it is as ethical ontology that her thinking has influenced later thinkers, and in particular the political and philosophical discussion in Italy.

The Spanish philosopher María Zambrano is one of those thinkers about whom one can say that her works encompass the better part of the historical changes of the twentieth century. Her life was severely affected by the politics of the century, with the Spanish Civil War and the Second World War forcing her into a forty-seven year exile from Spain. This article traces the background to the development of an ethical ontology – Zambrano calls it the ethics of history – and it is her contribution to the post-modern discussion of political community. A comprehensive analysis of Zambrano's works can be found in my book *Subjectivity from Exile – Place and Sign in the Works of María Zambrano* (Enquist Källgren 2015). The last fifteen years have seen increasing publication of Zambrano's works in Spanish, not to mention a growing interest in the USA. In London a recent conference on María Zambrano has paved the way for the publication and translation of her works into English. In Italy – where Zambrano lived for ten years – several contemporary philosophers, such as Adriana Cavarero and Roberto Esposito, draw explicitly on Zambrano's political thinking in their elaborations on political notions such as community (Esposito and Nancy 2010, 75–76; Esposito 2012) and universality (Cavarero 2000; Cavarero 2002; Cavarero, 2005). Nevertheless, Zambrano suffers the curious condition of having influenced contemporary political philosophy while remaining fairly unknown to a larger public. The analysis of Zambrano's ethical ontology can thus contribute to a better understanding of contemporary political philosophy as well as to the introduction of a little-known thinker to a larger and non-Spanish-speaking public. In my view, Zambrano's main contribution to contemporary philosophy is her development of a concept of individual subjectivity – an *ego* – that of necessity and fundamentally entails *the other*. Zambrano writes in *Persona y Democracia* (1958) in which one finds her most systematic political thinking, that her goal is to investigate the possibility of a society that does not sacrifice the individual (Zambrano 2014, 406–408). This can be understood as a *leitmotif* in all of Zambrano's writing on human subjectivity, and ever-present in her works (Enquist Källgren 2015, 264 and Andreu 2007, 56–62). In this sense, Zambrano's political and ethical thinking is comparable to that of, for example, Hanna Arendt and Simon Weil (Moreno Sanz 2014). My aim in this article is to discuss the relationship between the individual and the community as it is revealed in Zambrano's political texts. I will try to show that it is not in her reflection on political and social institutions that her works contribute to contemporary philosophy. Rather, her contribution lies in the claim that a democratic society cannot be reduced to institutions or voting processes and that it must be grounded in an ethical attitude that allows for both community and individual. From this perspective, and as opposed to those that only read her very early texts as political (Bundgård 2009), Zambrano's entire works is seen as profoundly political, as it is inscribed within the realm of her ethical ontology. Zambrano's explicitly political texts are full of common political concepts, which she redefines in order to create her own description of social and political reality. Particularly in her *Persona y Democracia* this leads to the development of the concept of *persona*, which Zambrano uses as a tool to describe her conception of a human subject that is both fundamentally individual and in community. In the following I will analyse some of the political concepts used by Zambrano, primarily *persona*, and show how they relate to her other works when discussed as an ethical ontology.

Zambrano's Political Context and Absolutism as a Problem

María Zambrano was born in Vélez-Málaga in southern Spain in 1904 and was educated as one of the first women at the Universidad Central (today Complutense) de Madrid. She studied philosophy and began her doctoral thesis in the seminar of Ortega y Gasset. In 1936 the Spanish Civil War broke out, and appointed as councillor of propaganda she defended the Republican government. At the end of the war, in 1939, she was forced to flee on foot over the Pyrenees and travelled shortly thereafter to Mexico, where several of the exiled Spanish intellectuals gathered. Zambrano spent over forty years in exile, travelling, writing and giving sporadic courses at universities in Latin America and Europe. She did not return to Spain until 1986, when she had already gathered quite a reputation, and received what is often called the Nobel Prize of the Spanish language, the Cervantes Literature Prize. She died in 1991.

The war put Zambrano in the strange position of being an exile, on the one hand maintaining her citizenship in Spain, but on the other hand without the possibility of returning for fear of prosecution. During the years of exile Zambrano constantly moved between countries, notably Mexico, Cuba, Puerto Rico, Italy and France, partly because she never obtained citizenship in any of the countries. This prevented her from having a steady job in the universities in, for example, Cuba. Even so, she knew and had contact with several of the European intellectuals, as José Ortega y Gasset, Elémire Zolla, Albert Camus (as it happens, Camus died in a car accident in 1960 with the manuscript of Zambrano's *El Hombre y lo Divino* in the car) and Emile Cioran. In Latin America both her philosophical and her political thinking have been influential, the latter more specifically in the development of the educational system of Puerto Rico, and to some extent in the formulations in its constitution (Fenoy Gutiérrez 2008, 32–34). Zambrano spent several years in Puerto Rico and was invited by the Governor, Luis Muñoz Marín, to collaborate in the ambitious project of education that he led after Puerto Rico's independence in 1955. In Cuba, Zambrano was a front figure in the new literary tradition during the fifties and sixties, side by side with José Lezama Lima and the *Orígenes* group (Vitier 1994, 85; Lezama Lima 2006, 185).

Zambrano's main political works (published between 1930 and 1958), heavily influenced by her experiences of the Civil War and the questions that gave it fuel, begin with the affirmation that in Europe there are two systems of ideas working against each other. The fascist system, based on a certain conception of the individual, stands against a communist system that tries to eradicate the individual. In her first book on politics, *Horizonte del liberalismo* (1930), Zambrano opposes both liberalism and communism and concludes that neither can sufficiently satisfy man's fundamental right to liberty.

Zambrano was accused repeatedly of being a communist, something she always refuted (Andreu 2002, 363). On the other hand, she was also accused of being a fascist in the years before the Spanish Civil War. She refuted that

accusation by arranging her own public trial, in which important intellectuals in Madrid stepped forward to defend her innocence (Moreno Sanz 2004,
683). In the light of her political thinking, even when taking into consideration what she wrote during the Civil War, there is no evidence to hold that
she was either a communist or a fascist. She was a fervent supporter of the
Spanish Second Republic, a revolutionary project that she did not conceive
of as communism. In her book on the role of the intellectual in the Spanish
Civil War, from 1937, Zambrano writes that even though one has to accept
the fact of a revolution, one does not need to accept all of its ideas (Zambrano 2015). In the introduction to the second edition from 1977, Zambrano
writes that the war must be conceived of as a war against a sacrificial history.
Considering the deaths of those defending Spain and Europe against fascism, that war should have been won once and for all, but it was not (Zambrano 2015, 132–34). In the introduction, Zambrano expresses the view that
a real revolution can only come about when the old notions of individual and
community are changed.

There is a direct correspondence between Zambrano's attempt to find
a third way in the political polarization during the Spanish Republic, and
the attempt in her political reflection to confront the problem of absolutism. In *Persona y Democracia* Zambrano deals with the problem of absolutism
by confronting individualism with the idea of an absolute state-society. The
problem is the fundamental idea in both the fascist and the communistic
system that it is possible to create a society so perfectly adapted to the essence
or nature of the human being that it is stable and beyond time (Zambrano
2011a, 442). The eschatological belief in the creation of a society beyond historic change – the absolute state or communist egalitarianism – creates a
society that demands human sacrifice, since there is no natural or essential
individual that does not live change. This suggests that the reason why history
occurs is not that we have yet to find the perfect organization in which time
and being are fulfilled. Rather, "man is a creature transiting a continuous
birth" (Zambrano 2011a, 459). Totalitarian societies ask for the sacrifice of
individuality based on the belief that it is possible to create a pure organization of society, in which the essential human being can find its place in an
absolute identification (Zambrano 2011a, 464–65). The belief in a fulfilled
and perfectly organized society is only possible if we assume that the human
being has some essential traits that should be reflected in the organization of
society. Zambrano's critique of absolutism carries with it a critique of human
essentialism. And while every attempt to think society as a structure that cor-

responds to what the human being *is* will fail and become totalitarian, Zambrano proposes the difficult task of thinking a society that safeguards the right to change.

Zambrano suggests that instead of a tragic history in which the human being continuously fails to build the perfect society to end all time – paradise on earth – what is needed is an ethical history (Zambrano 2011a, 418). She writes that a democratic society can only be legitimate as long as it ensures the liberty for rebirth (Zambrano 2011a, 499–501). The political actor in such a democratic society is not the individual but a subject that Zambrano calls *persona* (Zambrano 2011a, 474).

The argument is both confusing and tantalizing, since political rights and obligations are traditionally discussed precisely in terms of identity categories. Zambrano's thinking can be understood as an early attempt at questioning identity politics, and it can be placed alongside other attempts at thinking community without categories such as race, religion, nation or class. But Zambrano's thought is not intersectional, as could be, for example, the attempt at bypassing categorization by stating that individuals are always identified by a combination of categories, for example race, gender and class. For Zambrano, the most burning question of political philosophy is how to think the relationship between individual uniqueness or singularity, and the universality that is the fundament of society. In order to think a society that safeguards the possibility of change, Zambrano proposes a universalism that does not take for granted an essential similarity between the subjects of the community.

A Critique of the Liberal Individual

The relationship between uniqueness and community in Zambrano's political thinking can be rephrased in two questions that Zambrano repeatedly and explicitly worked with: (i) How can community be thought without sacrificing the fundamental uniqueness of subjects? (ii) How can community be thought to ensure the possibility to live with *the other*? Both these questions had been raised by Zambrano's experiences during the Spanish Civil War, which she perceived as a sacrifice of the Spanish people in a war between groups that have become absolute opponents (Zambrano 1998, 168–69; Zambrano 2011b, 220). In order to answer these questions Zambrano discusses the origin of society, drawing on Aristotle rather than the liberal contract theorists. When discussing the contract theory of classical liberal theory, Zambrano is in fact criticizing the idea that it is possible to think the individual outside of society. In other words, the individual must be thought of as the product of social interaction.

For the first liberal thinkers such as Locke and Rousseau, man's liberty was conceived as a natural liberty. In the natural stage, before society, man's freedom was absolute, only circumscribed by the lack of satisfaction of needs and desires, or by the needs and desires of others more powerful than oneself. It was only when agreeing, by means of a contract, to limit the individual's absolute liberty, that society could be established. According to Zambrano, criticizing Rousseau, society is not the product of a contract between free individuals – and consequently there can never have been a natural positive freedom, as in the right to satisfaction of needs and desires through surrounding nature (Zambrano 2011a, 449). Instead, the individual and his individual autonomy are the products of a historic development in the Greek city-states in which unique subjects become invested with a unique value and the power to act politically (Zambrano 2011a, 459).

The human being cannot be understood separately from society, and it is in society, not in the relationship to nature, that he first finds his true being, his *ser* (Zambrano 2011a, 454). The idea of man's intimate relationship to nature is only later in history a sign of man discovering his individuality. In fact, the first step to discovering individuality is a tribe's separation from the gods, the discovery that the gods do not always attend to prayers or sacrifices and that man is alone (Zambrano 2011a, 454–55). Zambrano elaborates on the same theme in *El hombre y lo Divino* (1955), where she explains how the experience of being an individual involves the notion of separation between *the ego* and the gods. This can only be produced when human needs and desires are disappointed, either by lack of necessities or by a feeling of not being answered in prayer. The individual has never lived in nature, but the individual is the product of man's experience of separation from nature, and the separation from the gods that surround him (Zambrano 2011a, 110–20).

Instead of a first natural stage Zambrano proposes a first sacred stage, in which the presence of the gods upholds a universal unity in the group worshipping them. History, and the development of the individual through a historical process, must then be understood as a process of turning pagan. And it is this "paganization" that permits the perception of the idea of the human being's intimacy with nature, at the same time as it constructs him or her as fundamentally different from that same nature – the human being takes the gods' place – and from any other human in the surroundings. This is the historical emergence of the human being's individuality. The individual is a product of historical change in which *the ego* and *the other* are produced as inner limits in what is already necessarily a society. This process is described similarly in *El Hombre y lo Divino* and in *Persona y Democracia,* both published during the fifties (Zambrano 2011a, 105–109, 204–208, 251–54 and Zambrano 2011a, 445–53).

In this description of the historical development of the individual, there is a tension between, on the one hand, cultural or historical dependency, and on the other hand transformation and creation. Society and the individual emerge at the same time, as two necessary parts of the human condition. It may be noted that Zambrano uses this expression – *la condición humana* – independently of Arendt, since *Persona y Democracia* was published in 1958 and written during the preceding years. When the individual, invested with political authority, acts, he or she does so in relation to that society by which the human being is individualized. This is why one cannot completely break with tradition; even a revolution is only possible on the grounds of a historical configuration of society, i.e. tradition. And, what is more, Zambrano concludes that it is not because of traditionalists or conservatives that tradition is maintained, which makes them superfluous. Tradition is maintained in every act of creation, she holds (Zambrano 2011a, 470–71).

By retelling the history of the development of the liberal conception of individuality, Zambrano points to what can be considered the basis for her own ethical ontology. The individual subject is dependent on the other as an inner limit of the larger whole that is society. When we think *ego* we must immediately think society. That is to say, the natural human place is in society. And, for a society in which the individual is to be possible at all, it cannot be built on the fundaments of a divinity. The unique individual is necessarily pagan.

The individual as an inner limit in a larger historical development could be interpreted as a kind of Hegelianism, but Zambrano in fact criticizes Hegel for wanting to reduce everything to one being in historical emergence (Zambrano 2011a, 102–105). It is precisely this that her critique of essentialism aims at. There is no essential human being, represented in one or other political system, and there is no God or absolute ideals to maintain the order of the world. The human being is subjected to constant historical and personal transformation, and given that this is so, there must be something else that founds its being as both individual and society. I will argue that Zambrano finds this foundation in ethics.

Individuo and Persona: The Construction of an Ethical Subject

The concept of *persona* can probably be conceived of as Zambrano's most important political contribution. With it Zambrano distinguishes between the particular part of human being that is in history and in community, and the nucleus that is the universal foundation or possibility of human community. Her contribution lies in conceiving of this universal foundation as a human function that is valid in any human historical circumstance. And by describing this function as creating and recreating individuality and otherness, it becomes necessarily ethical.

For Zambrano, the individual can be described based on two dimensions of its being. On the one hand, the aspect that describes the particular historical or cultural circumstances in which the human being lives, and on the other hand, that aspect which can be understood as the structure that universally defines individual being. In its first aspect the human being is always historicized, it is susceptible to change – in fact, time is one of its fundamental elements as man turns towards the future – but it is also the carrier of tradition and meaning. In the second aspect the human being cannot be historicized and is therefore not susceptible to change; it is the universal part of man, both in the sense of independence from time and in the sense of being present in every human being. Of this latter aspect can we say that it is a transcendental part of the human being, but still only possible to conceive within the human lived life, and as such ontological. Zambrano calls the first aspect *individuo* and the second *persona*.

> The place of the *individuo* is society, but the place of the *persona* is an intimate space. And in that, yes, resides an absolute. Not in any other place of the human reality. Nothing that has been in us, nothing that is our product is absolute nor can be so. Only that unknown and without name, that which is loneliness and liberty [is absolute]. (Zambrano 2011a, 467)

The two perspectives constitute the relationship between the particular and the universal in Zambrano. The human being is never only placed in history and culture, nor can it be reduced to certain universal principles or transcendental *a priori*'s. It is the relationship between particular and universal – between *individuo* and *persona* – in its specific historical variation that compounds the individual.

Importantly, Zambrano's *persona* has a universal function: it allows every man to be conscious of his own being and thus transcend it. She writes in *El hombre y lo Divino* that the *persona* is the part of the human being that survives destruction, and she connects it to hope (Zambrano 2011a, 257). Similarly, in *Persona y Democracia*, she writes that the *persona* is a continuous transcending and opening up towards the future. It is emptiness, *vacío*, that continuously fills and is given form in new configurations. Zambrano writes that "the *persona* reveals itself to itself and it is like the place from which reality is revealed, appears" (Zambrano 2011a, 468). Being a *persona* also means being conscious of the responsibility implied by creation towards the future and towards others. In fact, it is only when we grow conscious of the responsibility inherent in the privilege to be singular and in creation that we become *personas*. The construction of the human being as both *individuo* and *persona* plays an important role for how Zambrano understands community and democracy. "The fact that history exists depends on the fact that because there is a society there is a past, and because man is persona there is a future" (Zambrano 2011a, 473). If the human being is both individual in its historical and community interaction, and universally singular as a *persona*, then it is between these two aspects of the human being that the possibility of living with the other emerges. I.e., it is because the human being has both these aspects that it is possible to perceive and live with the other at all. According to Zambrano, the most important limit or border for a new conception of democracy is not the national border, but the inner limit by which the individuals become *personas*, i.e. ethical and political subjects (Zambrano 2011a, 491).

The *individuo* is the part of man where history takes place, where tradition and beliefs create the specific situation in which man exists. The *persona* is that place with which we think, reflect and, according to Zambrano, transform. The *persona* executes a stepping back, or distancing itself from the cultural belonging in which it, through that same distancing movement, experiences itself as *individuo* (Zambrano 2011a, 472–73). In a classic example of dialectics, the *persona's* stepping back or distancing itself is what creates the possibility of the experience of the *individuo*. It is the universal *persona* that lets us see our selves as *individuo*, in society, belonging to something and different from someone *other*. It is our own, internal difference which permits our experience of *the other*. "So, paradoxically history exists, this incessant change, because the human being, its protagonist, is something that is not encompassed in history, because in some dimension of its being [the human being] is beyond it" (Zambrano 2011a, 459). It is from the *persona* that we experience a gap between society and "I". The *persona* is the function that

allows for man to see himself in his situation as an *individuo*, because it separates him from the immediate presence of his surroundings, including the
other (Zambrano 2011a, 464). The *persona* is experienced as a fundamental
nothing – a room – in which anything can be dreamt, thought or desired, and
in this sense completely free (Zambrano 2011a, 468). But as soon as thought,
dream or desires are to be effectuated they immediately become placed in
history, and thereby bound by the necessities of the historical or cultural situation. In this sense the relationship between *individuo* and *persona* shows the
two most fundamental characteristics of man: the ability to transcend any
unit or situation presently at hand paired with the demand that I make the
other present before me (Zambrano 2011a, 468). The space of the *persona* is
not only the space in which man re-creates himself as *ego*, but also the space
in which he must demand and re-create the presence of the other.

Zambrano's distinction between *individuo* and *persona* suggests that the
human being is a political subject in so far as he or she can step back from the
historical circumstances and discover itself as different to itself, and hence
possible to transform. This transformation will, however, lead to new historical circumstances; there is no transformation without configuration of society. This is why there is a human history. The movement of the *persona* in relationship to the *individuo*, the recreation of a proper inner limit suggests the
possibility of transformation that can only be acted out in history, in society.
The inner limit is conceived of as creative, and necessary, in the sense that
without it, human transformation would be impossible. While it upholds otherness, it is also the sign of precisely that which is universal in man, the movement by which he recreates himself continuously in history. To experience
myself as an individual is necessarily to experience the other as a process of
transformation precisely because the other is fundamentally tended between
individuality and universality. In this its human condition, the other is also
fundamentally similar.

Zambrano's argument is that it is by perceiving one's own singularity in continuous transformation that it is possible to perceive the other. Without ego
there can be no other. However, the opposite is also true. Without other there
could be no ego. It is in the reflective interaction between the *individuo* and
persona that community comes about since it is here that the other is engaged
in my very own process of transformation. Society is based on the relationship
to the world that allows for the *persona* to distinguish itself as singular in relation to somebody other, yet similar because in doing so it must allow for the
other to be equally singular and in a similar transformative process. Ethics is

invested with ontological necessity in Zambrano's description of the human community, as the basis of the distinction between *individuo* and *persona*. Ethics consists of recognizing the other's singularity as a political subject, at the same time as it recognizes its necessary engagement in the development of a proper singular and political subjectivity.

It can be noted that hidden in this discussion are notions of political liberty and dependency, again placed in an ontological discussion. In *Persona y Democracia* Zambrano wrote that what characterized the *persona* was the consciousness of its own creative liberty and responsibility. In *El Hombre y lo Divino* identity is equated with liberty as the result of the other's gaze.

> The vision liberates life, and the vision of oneself brings the highest degree of liberty. But if the vision of oneself is not direct but reflected through the other, the liberty is acquired by means of the other. We are, in effect, through and by the other and with him. / Liberty is identity. It seems as if the goal towards which life tends is that which in modern philosophical language has been called 'subject', the formation of a subject; and subject is identity. (Zambrano 2011a, 282)

In this quotation human liberty lies in the recognition of *the other* as a similar, which just like the *ego* has the capacity to see. And while the subject gains identity and subjecthood through the gaze of the other, one must assume that it is the recognizing, i.e. the vision of the other, that lets it in turn be identified. Zambrano's argumentation underlines the interdependency that liberty has with society. It stresses the relationship between inside and outside, or the limit as point of identification. In this sense not only individual identity is important; also crucial is *the other* that we neither can control nor understand completely, i.e. society. In *Persona y Democracia* history that takes the place of *the other*, as the situated circumstances of human life. In *El Hombre y lo Divino*, Zambrano refers to *the other*, as all kinds of beings we cannot understand, including all organic life (Zambrano 2011a, 227). Similarly, Zambrano exemplifies in *Persona y Democracia* the attitude one needs to take towards *the other*, when considered as a *persona*, with the relation to someone that we cannot understand. The relationship to *the other* in Zambrano's works is fundamentally a relationship with somebody that we cannot control or know. Likewise, in her works on exile, foremost *Los Bienaventurados* (1991), the other is depicted in the image of a great and unknown desert that as an ocean forces itself down the throat of the exile inverting inner and outer, and creating subjectivity as inner difference (Zambrano 2003, 35–36). In this book, the solution to the problem of being taken over by *the other*, inverted and annihilated by the fact of not recognizing either one's own inside or the other's outside is to find a common homeland (Zambrano 2003, 41–43). Zambrano's discussion further stresses that without difference there would be no liberty, and while the individual is free to turn in any direction it is precisely because it has to make present and be affected by *others* that it can transcend and transform itself.

The repression and fixation of the *persona* is the main problem in absolute societies of any ideology, according to Zambrano, and in her view only democracy can assure the free movement between *individuo* and *persona*. For that reason she elaborates at length in *Persona y Democracia* on the organization of a democratic society. What is most striking about reflection is her repeated emphasis that democracy must assure an ethical organization of society. Whereas Zambrano's views of democratic institutions are problematic and open for critique from various perspectives, the discussion brings with it a profound reflection on otherness, similarity and recognition that criticizes the idea of a liberating identity politics.

Democracy as an Ethical Order

Zambrano advocates a society that is based on the persona, and not on the individual. A democratic society must be organized so as to admit the continuous change and recreation performed by the persona, and not on the temporary place occupied by the individual. Democracy entails the recognition of the other as somebody that cannot be known, hence not categorized or forced to identify. Democracy should be a system that assures the right to be other if we are to follow Zambrano's argument, and this is a normative statement. Zambrano writes that democracy is the regime of the unity of multiplicity, and therefore, it recognizes every diversity, every difference in situation. (Zambrano 2011a, 498)

Recognizing every difference means for Zambrano recognizing anyone in his or her particular historical situation. She writes that the present is never only my present, but the multiplicity of perspectives constituted by individuals, groups and even classes. But this does not mean that culture is a legitimate argumentation for specific rights. A democratic structure that recognizes diversity recognizes an individual's situation only as a point of departure from which he or she will become something else. To recognize somebody as *other* is consequently not only to recognize him or her as *individuo*, but also to recognize them as *personas*.

> And that equality of all men, a fundamental "dogma" of the democratic faith, is equality in as far as they are human personas, not because of their qualities or character, equality is not the same as being uniform. (Zambrano 2011a, 501)

A democratic structure should not protect any particular historical or cultural circumstance as such, even though one must remember and let history be visible as a temporary situation from which the future will emerge. Any historical or cultural expression is only the sign of something universal – the transformation towards the future – and must be conceived of as a necessary part of the movement that transforms society, with its necessary implication of the other. Historical and cultural circumstances are the point of departure, the means by which we concede the other place so that it is possible for him and ourselves to transform. Therefore, to connect specific rights to specific cultural or class expressions would be to commit the same crime as absolutism, namely to lock a person into a historically temporary situation that is in reality only viable for a short range of time, and that would consequently prevent the individual from his basic right: to transform.

Zambrano's discussion constantly underlines that the democratic state must make possible the coexistence of *others* and that its main object is to conserve the possibility of every individual to change what he is. In this sense democracy is constituted by a political abandonment of sacrificial history. The fundamental ethical obligation found in Zambrano's works is to construct society in such a manner as to let the other have a historical or cultural place only to transcend it. Recognizing the other is thus not only recognizing him as an *individuo* – placed in history or society – but also recognizing him as *persona*, or as essentially transcending any present situation. Recognizing the other is recognizing him in his multiple being, in his possibilities. This suggests that the basic right of man is in fact the right not to be categorized and not to be identified. The foundation of political legitimacy is the recognition of the other as stemming from the same expressive and transcending function, not as an identifiable entity to which rights and prohibitions can be adduced. The ethical attitude is to understand that being is temporary expression and can never be reduced to categories of race, ethnicity or sex, for example. And, politics is played out as integration in the social space of temporary historical expressions, driven by the *persona* as foundational political agent. The ever-changing *persona* is constantly integrating in the sense that subject transformations are only possible in relation to others. One's own process of identification integrates the other, necessarily. Democracy, here understood as a performative process rather than a system of institutions, is to make the political subjects conscious of their responsibility to make present the expressions – for example political claims – emerging from *the others*. Zambrano's ethical ontology is politically relevant precisely because it thinks the relation between the subject and community by questioning the liberal individual as the main political actor. Doing so, it nevertheless sacrifices the possibility of thinking the "absolute other" as *the other* is converted into a similar. Difference is placed in the *individuo,* and similarity in the functions of the transformative and creating *persona.* This is probably Zambrano's most relevant contribution; the insistence that being similar is not being similar in any essential sense; similarity lies in the function or necessity to express being.

The discussion on the organization of society that Zambrano conducts is aimed at the possibility of thinking a political structure in which the claims from *the other* can be received. At the end of *Persona y Democracia,* Zambrano performs what can be read as a class analysis in relation to her conception of democracy. Drawing heavily on José Ortega y Gasset's *La rebelión de las masas* (1930), Zambrano develops concepts such as *pueblo,* people, *masas,* the masses, and *minorías,* minorities. The latter is the concept that she proposes as a means of organizing society beyond class conflicts, and it is at least partially opposed to Ortega's masses (Ortega y Gasset 1984). Zambrano refers explicitly to Ortega's book, and writes that with the concept of masses the author made explicit a condition of industrialized society (Zambrano 2011a, 485). The concept is not to be understood as Marxist. Concepts such as "masses" and "people" had their own particular flavor between the liberals in Spain before the Civil War. The concept of "people" was often connected to traditional ways of life, often in the countryside, whereas the "masses" were the problematic result of industrialized society (Ouimette 1998).

In Zambrano's description, the masses are people only interested in enjoying rights and benefits. They are consumers who live on the products of industrialized society but who do not know either how to produce (or controls the means of production) or how to be spiritually creative. And worst of all, she writes, they do not care (Zambrano 2011a, 485). The masses is a concept describing a way of living, and as such it is distinguished from the people, according to Zambrano, which is "radical reality" (Zambrano 2011a, 478).

The people are that unknown and undescribable material – "life without texture" (Zambrano 2011a, 213) – from which authority and society ultimately derive. It can also be passive, however, and the victim of demagogy, something that in the end risks leading to totalitarianism. She exemplifies with the development of Nazi power in Germany (Zambrano 2011a, 495). Zambrano's own concept of minorities – also inspired by Ortega y Gasset (1984, 103–108) – is a concept that proposes a way of leading the continuous movement and transformation of the people in a positive direction. The ideal is an intellectual elite that can "direct their [the people's] satisfactions" (Zambrano 2011a, 491). As opposed to those minorities organized around emotion – again she uses the Nazi movement as an example – the minorities recognized in democracy are minorities organized around interest, i.e. interest groups. According to Zambrano, these are the only groups that can transform society, not for example classes (Zambrano 2011a, 492).

Zambrano's Political Legacy – Concluding Discussion

However, the possibility to freely form minority groups seems somewhat inadequate in relation to the overall problem of a sacrificial history and society as identified by Zambrano. Even if we take into consideration the comments in passing about the need for the democratic society to take care of basic biological needs, such issues as distribution of power, and economic equality are completely overlooked in Zambrano's account of democracy. To her, the important discussion of democracy lies on an ontological level, and not in the distribution of power. This also makes her analyses of social groups and institutions halt, to say the least.

The lack of a discussion of economic and political power is consistent with earlier parts of her political works, and it can partly be explained by the contexts in which they were written. It is known that Zambrano formed part of a group of young students who in 1932 drafted a political manifesto criticizing the political activities undertaken by the then Republican government. The manifesto bore a strong resemblance to Zambrano's *Horizontes del liberalismo*, but she would soon withdraw support from the text that she found drawing too close to fascist corporatism (Moreno Sanz 2015, 40–46). *Horizontes del liberalismo* nevertheless discussed a material transformation and spiritual organization of society, which she speaks of in terms of a renovation of science, art, technology and philosophy (Moreno Sanz 2015, 15). Not in terms of, for example, economic equality. As both Bundgård and Moreno Sanz argue, there is a direct relationship between Zambrano's early political thinking and the debates and political landscape in Madrid before the Civil War, particularly in relation to Ortega (Bundgård 2009; Moreno Sanz, 2015). This could explain why Zambrano conceives of democracy and politics in the terms that she does. But *Persona y Democracia* was published in 1958, a time in which the political landscape in both Spain and Europe had completely changed.

As Sebastián Fenoy Gutiérrez emphasizes, *Persona y Democracia* has to be read in direct relation to the political debates about independence in Puerto Rico (Fenoy Gutiérrez 2008). Zambrano was a close friend of Luis Muñoz Marín, the Puerto Rican governor during the fifties and the man who wrote large parts of the new Puerto Rican Constitution, ratified in 1952 and proclaiming Puerto Rico a free state. *Persona y Democracia* was ordered and published by Muñoz Marín, who also employed Zambrano as a writer in the journals of the Puerto Rican ministry of education (Fenoy Gutiérrez 2005). Jesús Moreno Sanz points to several direct text coincidences between the Puerto Rican Constitution and *Persona y Democracia* (Moreno Sanz 2004, 282–84). One can find traces of the proximity between Zambrano's thought and Muñoz Marín's political stances in the latter's personal archive, in the form of notes entitled "Pensando en la democracia con María Zambrano" (Abellán 2001). From this perspective Zambrano's political thinking can be understood more as an elaboration of principles than as an actual political proposal. And Zambrano could have felt she had the opportunity to continue in Puerto Rico what she was not able to do in Spain, because of the Civil War. In fact, the Civil War was an important issue in Puerto Rico too, dividing society into pro-Franco conservatives and republicans (Albert 1992). Even though these were by no means the only political conflicts in Puerto Rico at the time (and maybe not even the most important ones) they affected Zambrano directly, and she may have felt the need to ensure that the political crisis in Spain and Europe, pitting different ideologies against each other, would not be repeated in the new state.

Other publications from Zambrano's time in Latin America corroborate that Zambrano understood the Latin American states as the consciousness that could save the democratic principles in the light of a Europe in crisis (Zambrano 1943). In addition, Zambrano understood the secluded condition of islands as the paradisiacal image of rebirth (Zambrano 1940). From a political point of view these conditions of rebirth could very well be likened to the Greek *polis*, at least in the sense of being a small political entity. If the individual was born out of the Greek *polis*, why could the *persona* not be born out of the Puerto Rican progress towards democracy? The lack of discussions on power and economic equality can in part be explained by the fact that Zambrano wrote in close relation to an educated and political elite – in the case of both the Spanish Republic and Puerto Rico. She was a professed liberal with a profound belief in the value of the human individual, and in the light of the totalitarian regimes where she lived, she wanted to think the possibilities of a community that would not sacrifice the individual. In this sense the lack of a discussion on the economic and power relations of the twentieth century can in addition be explained by her interest in extrapolating universal historical traits from European history and in finding universally valid solutions.

In consequence, it is the discussion that I have repeatedly referred to as Zambrano's ethical ontology that has had an impact on contemporary political thinkers, such as Adriana Cavarero and Roberto Esposito. The latter's book *The Third Person*, begins its critique of the western construction of human rights and human value with a direct critique of Zambrano's concept of *persona* (Esposito 2012, 1). Esposito cites Zambrano's *Persona y Democracia* as a primary example of what he understands as a problematic western belief in an irreducible human individual. What Esposito is criticizing is the idea that a concept like person could bridge the gap between the individual and community.

To the extent that Zambrano's concept of *persona* is understood as a fundamental principle of democracy, as exposed in *Persona y Democracia*, there are reasons to agree with Esposito that it is problematic. As we have seen, the concept of *persona* entails a separation into *ego* and *other* without which neither community nor individuality can occur. The very solution to the problem of the relation between individual and community is continuously reiterating the same dichotomies. This reiteration of dichotomies lies at the heart of the critique in Esposito's book (Esposito 2012, 15).

What Esposito is discussing is in fact an issue that Zambrano – I hold – addressed in several of her later works, most importantly in *Claros del Bosque* and *Notas de un método*, albeit not in political terms. Esposito's intent to found the human being as a political being in a concept of non-person takes as its departure the linguistic investigations of Émile Benveniste. Similarly, Zambrano elaborates on what can be understood an ethics of the symbol in her very late publication. What Esposito – and Zambrano for that matter – describe as a gap between individual and community, between *ego* and *other,* Zambrano tries to bridge with the help of ethics. In fact, as against Esposito's interpretation of her works, Zambrano held that it is the human being's tragic condition to be always torn between individuality and community, between transcendental functions and historical place.

Adriana Cavarero draws explicitly on Zambrano for a solution to the problem of the relationship between the individual and community. In her *Towards a Philosophy of Vocal Expression*, it is the uniqueness of the human body and its expressions that come to form the basis for an at least possible political universality (Cavarero 2005). In a sense, one could say that what Esposito criticizes as regards Zambrano's notion of the *persona*, Cavarero in fact elaborates on, in terms of the voice as a bodily expressive uniqueness. This comes closer to how Zambrano herself treats individual identity in the larger part of her later works, except in *Persona y Democracia*, where the *persona* is the holder of a unique human function and in prolongation value. In Cavarero's work, the uniqueness of the individual human being is preserved not as a spiritual value, but as the bodily signs of subjectivity (Cavarero 2005, 1–16).

This argument makes the relation between *ego* and *other* easier to resolve since it places uniqueness in the very location where the *ego* meets the world, i.e. in the body. For both Cavarero and Esposito what is at stake is a formula that permits thinking "one-and-together" rather than "one-and-other" as the basis for social community. This is an attempt that they share with Zambrano, and which the two younger authors initiated, drawing on Zambrano. For all three authors the political questions of today must be addressed as ontology. In fact, Zambrano does not consider her *Persona y Democracia* a political treatise but describes it as the search for an "ethics of history" (Zambrano 2011a, 392). By way of conclusion it can be gathered that Zambrano's political thinking suggests a larger field of ethical ontological thinking that confronts the political problems of the twentieth century with a reflection on the conditions of being and ultimately the human condition. Zambrano can be related to more well-known authors, such as Martin Heidegger and Hanna Arendt. Zambrano's thinking is one way into a more contextualized reading of what is sometimes referred to as the Italian bio-political school of thought. Conclusively, and as has already been noted, this suggests that it is of the utmost relevance to further investigate Zambrano's writings as an ethical project.

References

Abellán, José Luis, 2001. *El exilio como constante y categoría*. Madrid: Biblioteca Nueva.

Albert, Matilde. 1992. *El exilio español en Puerto Rico*. La Coruña: Ediciones Do Castro.

Andreu, Agustín. 2007. *María Zambrano – el dios de su alma*. Granada: Editorial Comares.

Arendt, Hannah, 1994. *The Origins of Totalitarianism*. New York: Harcourt Books.

Bundgård, Ana. 2009. *Un compromiso apasionado*, Madrid: Trotta.

Cavarero, Adriana. 2005. *Towards a Philosophy of Vocal Expression*. Stanford: Stanford University Press.

Enquist Källgren, Karolina. 2015. *Subjectivity from Exile – Place and Sign in the Works of María Zambrano*. Doctoral diss. University of Gothenburg.

Esposito, Roberto. 2012. *The Third Person*. Cambridge: Polity Press.

Fenoy Gutiérrez, Sebastián. 2005. "María Zambrano en el departamento de instrucción pública puertoriqueño." In *Actas del Congreso Internacional del Centenario de María Zambrano*, 210–19. Vélez-Malaga: Fundación María Zambrano

———. 2008. *Los originales de María Zambrano*. Barcelona: Balmes Ediciones.

Moreno Sanz, Jesús. 2004. "Insúlas extrañas, lámparas de fuego: Las raíces espirituales en la política de Puerto Rico." In *María Zambrano: la visión más transparente*, edited by Juan Antonio González Fuentes and José María Beneyto Pérez. 209–86. Madrid: Trotta.

———. 2004. "Cronología y genealogía filosófico-espiritual." In *La Razón en la sombra – antología crítica María Zambrano*, edited by Jesús Moreno Sanz. 673–730. Madrid: Siruela.

———. 2014. *Edith Stein en compañía*. Madrid: Plaza y Valdéz

———. 2015. "Presentación de Horizontes del liberalismo." In *Obras Completas* vol. I. By María Zambrano. Edited by Jesús Moreno Sanz, 3–50. Barcelona: Galaxia Gutenberg.

Ortega y Gasset, José. 1984. *La rebelión de las masas*. Madrid: Espasa-Calpe.

Ouimette, Víctor, 1998. *Los intelectuales españoles y el naufragio del liberalismo (1923–1936)*. Valencia: Pre-textos.

Zambrano, María. 1940. *Isla de Puerto Rico*. Havana: La Verónica.

———. 1943. "Speech and Discussion." In *América ante la crisis mundial*. Havana: Comisión Cubana de Cooperación Intelectual.

———. 1992. *Horizontes del liberalismo (Nuevo liberalismo)*. Madrid: Ediciones Morata.

———. 1998. "Letter to Rafael Dieste 4 November 1937." In *Los intelectuales en el drama de España – Escritos de la Guerra Civil*, edited by Jesus Moreno Sanz, 168–69. Madrid: Trotta.

———. 2003. *Los Bienaventurados*. Madrid: Siruela.

———. 2011a. *Persona y Democracia. Obras Completas* vol. III. Barcelona: Galaxia Gutenberg.

———. 2011a. *El Hombre y lo Divino*. In *Obras Completas* vol. III. Barcelona: Galaxia Gutenberg.

———. 2011b. "Letter to José María Chacón y Calvo 4 March 1940." In *Escritos sobre Ortega*, edited by Ricardo Tejada, 220–21. Madrid: Trotta.

———. 2015. *Los intelectuales en el drama de España*. In *Obras Completas* vol. I. Barcelona: Galaxia Gutenberg.

Western Historical Narratives and Political Myths

Justifying a Just War in the Twenty-First Century

Maren Lytje[1]

Abstract

This article takes its point of departure in some of the historical narratives used in the justification of The War on Terror in the early 2000s. The article suggests that these might be conceptualized as political myth, suggesting further that previous conceptualizations of political myth face a conundrum: on one hand, political myth is perceived as a founding narrative of the state, on the other, myth itself is seen as a cognitive category which organizes experience. This conundrum leads the article to ask: 1) what is the relationship between myth as a cognitive category, and the political myth which legitimizes the rule of state or state-like groups; and 2) is this relationship between myth as a natural part of the human body and myth as a narrative discernible in the historical analogies and historical narratives used in the justification of warfare? In order to address these questions the article develops a theory of political myth based on Ernst Kantorowicz's work on medieval political theology in *The King's Two Bodies*. Based on an interpretation of Kantorowicz's work the article suggests that that political myth may be understood as a substitution game which wavers between the natural order of the human being itself and the political community. This substitution game is organized around a fantasy of sovereignty which mediates between these two aspects. The article then evaluates this definition of political myth in the context of two examples used in The War on Terror, one from a Danish and the second from an American context.

Introduction

The use of historical analogies in western state leaders' justifications of war is a well-known phenomenon. For example, in his address to the Congress on September 20, 2001 George W. Bush likened the attack on the World Trade Center to the Japanese bombardment of Pearl Harbor in 1941 and told his

---

1 Maren Lytje recently received a Ph.D. in history in the Department of Culture and Global Studies at Aalborg University.

audience that the terrorists followed "in the path of fascism, Nazism and totalitarianism" (Bush 2001, 65–75).[2] At a Labour conference on October 2, 2001 Tony Blair reminded his constituents of the importance of conducting an ethically responsible foreign policy. Ethically responsible meant similar to the one the New Labour government had conducted in Kosovo in 1999 with NATO's UN-sanctioned air bombardment of Yugoslav military installations. The "ethical" lay in the fact that military intervention had been instigated due to gross violations of human rights and ethnic cleansing rather than for geopolitical and strategic reasons (Blair 2001). In an article on the March 26, 2003 former General Secretary of NATO, then Prime Minister of Denmark, Anders Fogh Rasmussen compared Saddam Hussein to Adolf Hitler to drum up support for the war on Iraq.

Historical analogies are often embedded in presupposed or sometimes spelled-out historical narratives. For example, George W. Bush's reference to the United States' role in the Second World War was part of a well-known narrative about American exceptionalism (Esch 2010). Tony Blair's reference to the humanitarian intervention in Kosovo in 1998 and 1999 similarly implied a historical narrative about the development of British foreign affairs, from the supposedly realist politics of self-interest under Margaret Thatcher and John Major to an ethically responsible foreign politics, which was the hallmark of New Labor; and Anders Fogh Rasmussen's analogy between Hitler and Hussein was part of a spelled-out narrative about the history of Danish foreign affairs according to which Denmark had developed from a small state to an important ethical and military actor upholding civil liberties and human rights across the globe (Rasmussen 2003a).

In western academics, the use of historical analogies and their implied historical narratives are often studied within the framework of the invention of traditions school.[3] Here, scholars frequently interpret them as a prop of the state which forges one-dimensional and sometimes oppressive visions of social unity and history.[4] These visions can be used to legitimize war because they are assumed to be part of the collective memory of

2 Bush repeated this analogy in an address to the department of Defense Service of Remembrance in the Pentagon on October 11, 2001 (Bush 2001, 75–82) and again in an address to the UN where he emphasizes the crimes of the Holocaust (Bush 2001, 83–90).

3 For some of the founding texts of the invention of tradition school, see for example (Anderson 2006) and (Hobsbawm and Ranger 2012).

4 See, for example (Duara 1995).

the political community. On this reading, historical analogies and historical narratives assume the character of *political myths*: they are the founding stories of the state or state-like groups, and might function as the gloss of a state-sanctioned ideology which can obscure the force of executive power.[5]

While political myths can be interpreted as founding narratives of state (or state-like groups) which grant legitimacy to the state and thereby to the state's war efforts, myth itself is sometimes conceptualized as a cognitive category through which the mind organizes the world. As such, myth is engrained in the brain and therefore, we must assume part of the biological constitution of the human being. This discrepancy between political myth as a founding history and myth as a cognitive category is at play in one of the classical conceptualizations of myth formulated by the German idealist philosopher Ernest Cassirer's work. In *The Myth of the State* published posthumously in 1946, for example, Cassirer conceptualized political myth as the gloss of the executive power of the state. With the Arian myth fresh in mind, Cassirer argued that the primitiveness of myth could be used to veil the brute intentions of the state apparatus: political myth authorized the rule of state by endowing the state with a founding history which granted it temporal endurance and from which it drew its authority. However, in order to make this argument, Cassirer took his point of departure in his previous work on mythical thought from 1922: myth, he argued, could be a menace of the political realm because it was a symbolic form through which the human mind had to pass in order to reach maturity. As such, it was an indispensable part of the formative operations of consciousness through which the human being ascends from materiality

---

5 From this perspective, the Swedish political scientist, Jan Engstrom, for example, sees historical analogies as important tools of political rhetoric, which can make certain political responses seem inevitable (Angstrom 2011). Similarly, Aurélie Campana argues from a constructionist perspective that mythical narratives tell tales of the just struggle of the people against and oppressor, which can be used to legitimize war (Campana 2009). Yen Le Espiritu and Diana Wolf argue that the proliferation of the Holocaust in American war memories obscures the debate about the morally dubitable role of the United States in the Vietnam War. The focus on the Holocaust emphasizes the heroic nature of the US as the liberator of the world from evil, whereas focus on the Vietnam War would be more likely to emphasize the problem of American military power and hegemony in the world (Espiritu and Wolf 2013). The use of historical analogies is not the exclusive domain of pro-war politicians; they are equally used to instill anti-war sentiments, for example when American demonstrations against the war in Iraq resounded with references to the Vietnam War, which has a much muddier reputation in the American public. See for example (Bottici 2007).

to spirituality.[6] Adherence to a political myth was therefore a sign that the collective mind had become stuck in a primitive form of consciousness which enabled war-mongering and genocide, because it transferred the irrational sacred rituals of savage societies into the heart of what ought to be rational, modern politics (Cassirer 1946).

Cassirer's conceptualization of political myth as a menace of the political realm which sanctions warfare and oppression has recently been criticized by the political scientist, Chiara Bottici. In a comprehensive study of the concept of political myth, Bottici argues that Cassirer's approach to political myth is too one-dimensional: while political myth can justify war and prop up the powers that be, they can also be used to forge a common ground for people fighting oppression and injustice. Myth itself, Bottici argues, is value-free because it is a function of the human mind itself, which helps organize the political experience of different social groups (Bottici 2007, 15). As such it is a non-static category which changes in accordance with human experience. According to Bottici, political myth grounds a community by telling the story of its common, political experience thereby granting "significance to the political conditions and experiences of a social group" (Bottici and Challand 2010, 12). Political myth might justify the rule of state and thereby justify the state at war, for example by endowing the state with a founding history and consequent destiny; but it might as easily justify rising against a state which is seen as the illegitimate ruler of a social group.

While Bottici's flexible definition of political myth allows us to look at the recalcitrant functions of myth and adjust it to concrete, empirical analysis, she remains within Cassirer's framework in two important respects. Firstly, like Cassirer, Bottici suggests that political myth is related to the experience of being governed. Political myth gives temporal endurance to the rule of a social group, whether it is the rule of state, the rule of a group in opposition to the state, or to other groups. Secondly, Bottici shares Cassirer's assumption about the naturalness of myth. While she dismisses his developmental hier-

---

6 Ernest Cassirer proposed this theory as early as 1922 in his key work, *The Philosophy of Symbolic Forms: Mythical Thought*. In this work, Cassirer saw myth as the second of three symbolic forms through which the human mind had to pass in order to reach the maturity of the scientific mind. Cassirer's early work on myth was firmly embedded within the Comteian framework of the development of the scientific mindset and Hegelian-style philosophy of history: myth was more primitive than scientific thought, though it remained an important part of the processes of consciousness. Cassirer's philosophy of symbolic forms, however, is also indebted to Kant's critique of reason according to which the mind's formative operations decide how we perceive the thing-in-itself. Like Kant's categories, myth belongs to the formative operations of consciousness through which the "I" separates itself off from the world and the object. See e.g. Kant (2000, 3–53).

archy according to which myth is "primitive," it remains a cognitive category through which the human mind organizes the world. Myth is, in other words, part of the biological constitution of the human being, and while the historical narratives which "grant significance to the political experience of a social group" might be new or invented, myth itself is always, already there as part of the human brain.

The legitimizing function of political myth on one hand and the assumed naturalness of myth on the other, might lead two questions: Firstly, how does political myth authorize government, and how is that authorization related to war or war-like violence? For example, what authorizes the warfare of a democratically elected government? Secondly, the argument that myth is a cognitive category may lead to the question as to how myth can be always, already there, as an organizing principle engrained in the human brain? In the context of the justification of western war in the twenty-first century, these two questions may be rephrased in the following manner: firstly, what is the relationship between myth as a cognitive category which is always already there, and the political myth which legitimizes the rule of state or state-like groups and therefore can be used in the justification of warfare? Secondly, is this relationship between myth as a natural part of the human body and myth as a narrative discernible in the historical analogies and historical narratives used in the justification of warfare?

In answering these question, the article argues that the split in Cassirer and Bottici's works between myth as a cognitive category and myth as a founding story of the state or a social group in fact underpins the political myth itself: in the same way as myth wavers between referring to what is part of the natural constitution of the human being and a founding story, so the political myth wavers between what is considered the natural order of the human species and the order of the political community. The article further argues that the harmony between the two sides of the mythical coin is solved by means of a fantasy of sovereignty, which works towards founding the justice of the state at war. These arguments are made on the basis of an analysis of two of the examples of the use of political myth mentioned in the introductory paragraphs of the article, namely Anders Fogh Rasmussen's narrative of the development of Danish foreign affairs and George W. Bush's narrative of American exceptionalism.

The main questions of the article are addressed in the context of the justification of warfare in the twenty-first century. Similar questions have been raised in works focusing on different historical contexts, and the article first offers an interpretation of one of these works, namely Ernst Kantorowicz's *The King's Two Bodies: Studies in Medieval, Political Theology* (1957) which focuses the power constellation of the European Middle Ages and the sovereignty of kings. In interpreting *The King's Two Bodies*, the article emphasizes the fact that Kantorowicz himself placed the work in the trajectory of Cassirer's myth of state by suggesting that the Aryan myth of state might be seen as the last remnant of political theology. As such, Katorowicz's work on political theology might be seen as an often overlooked conceptualization of political myth. Political theology refers to a process of secularization whereby Catholic, theological concepts were transformed into political concepts which could sanction the rule of the secular state and justify the authority of the sovereign king. According to Kantorowicz, the gap between divine authority and secular rule was bridged by what he refers to as a "fiction of sovereignty," which transferred the justice of the natural order of the heavenly kingdom to the government of the state. Therefore, the article suggests that *The King's Two Bodies* might be seen as an example of the study of political myth, which directly addresses the relationship between the authority stemming from the natural order of things on one hand and the government of the earth on the other.

The interpretation of Kantorowicz is supplemented by a short interpretation of Hannah Arendt's *The Origins of Totalitarianism* (1951), a part of which focuses on the emergence of popular sovereignty in the seventeenth and eighteenth century Europe. In interpreting this part of Hannah Arendt's work, the article follows the American literary critic Eric Santner's suggestion that Hannah Arendt brings Kantorowicz's work further up to date. According to Arendt, the nation becomes heir to the semi-mysticism of the sovereign incorporation of the king's body, and hence functions as a "fiction of sovereignty" which binds the ruler (the state) to its source of authority (the people) and thereby legitimizes the rule of state.

In interpreting Kantorowicz's work on medieval political theology and Arendt's work on popular sovereignty, the article suggests that Kantorowicz's "fiction of sovereignty" functions as a fantasy in a psychoanalytical sense: the fiction of sovereignty does not designate the content of the political myth itself. Rather, it designates the organizing principle which orders the relationship between natural authority and earthly government. As a fantasy, the "fiction of sovereignty" sets in motion a substitution game between the two sides of the mythical coin: between the authority of a natural state which is always already there on one hand, and the secular rule of state on the other.

The article suggests that, interpreted in this manner, Kantorowicz's political theology offers an important and often overlooked contribution to the conceptualization of political myth by pointing the role that the "fiction of sovereignty" plays for the establishment of the political myth.

The article then asks if the theories developed by Kantorowicz and Arendt might still be relevant for understanding political myth in the twenty-first century, and it evaluates their theories in the context of Fogh Rasmussen's narrative of the development of Danish foreign affairs and Bush's narrative of American exceptionalism. In doing so, the article draws conclusions upon the continued relevance of Kantorowicz and Arendt's theories in the twenty-first century and proposes a concept of political myth which might be relevant for understanding the justification of western warfare in the twenty-first century.

Political Myth and Sovereignty: Kantorowicz with Arendt

The King's Two Bodies, published in 1957, is Ernst Kantorowicz's last published work. Kantorowicz was born in 1895 into a wealthy, bourgeois, non-practicing Jewish family in Poznan, and served in the German army during the Great War. After the war, he became affiliated with the romantic-conservative and later Nazi-leaning Georg Kreis, and his first published historical work from 1927, a biography of Frederik II, smacked of the "almost Romantic myth-making" later associated with the Nazi movement (Jordan 2007, xii). Kantorowicz himself, however, refused to take the oath to Adolf Hitler in 1934 and he left Germany in 1938 for the United States.

Kantorowicz's affiliation with an arch-conservative Romantic movement might explain why he placed his work in the trajectory of Cassirer's *Myth of State*: Cassirer was throughout his career a staunch adversary of the conservative romanticism that came to underpin the Nazi movement. However, while Cassirer might have provided the overall ideological sentiment for the *King's Two Bodies*, it was another thinker directly associated with the Nazi party who provided its intellectual grounds, namely Carl Schmitt.

In *The King's Two Bodies* Kantorowicz follows Carl Schmitt's famous maxim that "all significant concepts of the modern state are secularized theological concepts" (Schmitt 2005, 36). Consequently, he investigates how theological concepts were transformed into legal concepts which could sustain the justice of the secular ruler of the territorial state vis-à-vis the rule of the church. Kantorowicz takes his point of departure in the legal doctrine of the king's two bodies, his body public and his body private, conceptualized by English jurists in the sixteenth century (Kantorowicz 1997, 7–23). According to Kantorowicz, this doctrine can be traced back to early medieval notions of Christ-centered, liturgical kingship, which attempted to reconcile the "rule of the emperor" and "the rule of God." In early medieval conceptions of kingship, Kantorowicz says, the king was a Christ-like figure bound to the altar, and his link to the altar justified his earthly rule. During the high middle ages, however, the model of liturgical kingship developed into a juridical model according to which the king, like the Father, was the head of justice and thereby became linked to the just government of the world. According to the juridical model the king's body safeguarded the link between the rightful justice of the sovereign God on one hand and the administration of the earth on the other (Kantorowicz 1997, 42–60; 143).

The doctrine of the king's two bodies was meant to solve the gap between the king's mortality and his embodiment of the perpetuity of the territorial state. With a body private and a body politic the king embodied the individual as well as the species; and while his body private might die, his royal *dignitas* ensured the link between the mortal body of the king himself and his immortal powers on the other, between the king as an individual who died and the immortality of the species, which he represented. But the royal *dignitas* also bound the king as an individual to the administration of the state of which he was the head. Consequently, according to Kantorowicz, the perpetuity of the state did not lie in the king's body private, neither in his body politic, but rather in the sovereign cyphers and entitlements which linked the two.

Kantorowicz's study of medieval, political theology primarily pivots around legal documents and demonstrates how the legal framework of the secular, territorial state was influenced by theological concerns with administration of God's creatures. However, Kantorowicz's initial reference to Cassirer's myth of state indicates that his focus might not be on the justice of state but rather on the justification of the political power of the sovereign. However, justification in this context is neither the primitivism of Cassirer's political myth, nor is it simply the cunning manipulation of political elites. Rather, justification refers to a relationship between just, holy authority and just, secular administration. As such, it refers to a transition from a natural order laid down in accordance with the principles of the just authority, and the administration of secular life in accordance with the same principles. In Kantorowicz's work, then, "justification" is equivalent to what he terms a "fiction of sovereignty" which organizes the relationship between just authority and earthly rule. We could also use a Foucauldian vocabulary here and say that the fiction of sovereignty operates the gap between sovereignty and governmentality.[7] As we shall see in the analyses of Fogh Rasmussen's narrative of the development of Danish foreign affairs and Bush's narrative of American exceptionalism, these are similarly underpinned by a fiction of sovereignty which organizes the relationship between what is considered a natural order on one hand and the rule of the polity on the other.

Kantorowicz ends his work with an investigation of what he calls "man-centered" conceptions of kingship according to which *homo* rather than the king as head of the state of justice becomes the instrument for the development of *humanitas* (Kantorowicz 451). These developments, Kantorowicz argues, mark the end of the divinely sanctioned sovereignty of kings and the beginning of popular sovereignty. While Kantorowicz takes note of this transition, his study stops short of investigating how the divinely sanctioned sovereignty of kings has seeped into conceptions of popular sovereignty. However, the American, critical theorist, Eric Santner has suggested that we might use Hannah Arendt's *The Origins of Totalitarianism* to think through this transition (Santner 2011, 55–58).

In *Origins of Totalitarianism*, Arendt argues that the idea of the "nation" as it emerges in eighteenth- and nineteenth-century Europe is heir to the semi-mysticism of the king's body. According to Arendt, the nation stands in an adversary relationship to the state: the state administers in accordance with a natural rights philosophy, which grants equal status to all human beings pure and simple. Human rights, the right of man, therefore become the *raison d'être* of the "people" incorporated in the state. On the other hand, these rights are always inscribed in the particularity of the nation which stands above them (Arendt 1994, 290–302). In Arendt's conceptualization of popular sovereignty we may discern a remnant of Kantrowicz two-bodied king. Like the king the people have "two bodies," one which belongs to the human being in its natural state, the other which is invested with the insignias of belonging to a particular state. These two bodies are joined together through the fantasy of the nation which invests the human being in its natural state with the insignias of belonging to the political community incorporated in the state. By way of the nation, the people have access to the state

---

7 Michel Foucault suggests that the eighteenth century sees the waning of the sovereign power of the king and the emergence of governmental techniques whereby the state seeks to administer the life functions of its populations. These techniques are referred to as governmentality and the new power constellation as bio-power. Where sovereign power was tied to the law, the symbolic bond of blood, and the right to judge and to take life, bio-power concerns itself only with the production and sustenance of organic life processes. See (Foucault 2008) and (Foucault 1998).

which supposedly reflects the "will of the people," and administers the earth in accordance with the natural principles of the human being pure and simple.

While Kantorowicz indicates that political myth is propagandistic in nature by placing his work in the trajectory of Cassirer's *Myth of State*, the above interpretation of his work suggests that it might be opened up towards a definition of political myth, which neither consigns it to the function of state propaganda, nor to the biological function of cognitive processes. Rather, based on the above interpretation of Kantorowicz and Arendt, the article suggests that political myth may be understood as a substitution game which wavers between the natural order of the human being itself and the political community. This substitution game is organized around a fantasy of sovereignty, which mediates between the human being in its natural state and the political subject invested with the insignias of belonging to a political community. We might therefore understand political myth in the following sense: it is a story which continuously wavers between the human being in its natural order and the way of life of the political community, for example, in the context of popular sovereignty the political myth wavers between the natural rights of the human being pure and simple and the state. The political myth, however, is underpinned by a fantasy of the sovereign which mediates between the two sides of the political myth. In Arendt's case the fantasy of the nation mediates between the human being pure and simple and the citizen of the state, in Kantorowicz case the fantasy of the king's two bodies incorporated in his *dignitas* mediates between the kingdom of god and the administration of the earth.

While the above definition of myth is not developed specifically within the context of the justification of war, it is still relevant for addressing war. As suggested in the introduction of this article, the use of historical analogies and historical narratives in the justification of warfare might be addressed within the context of political myth; and while those who justify warfare do not necessarily take recourse to political myth, those which seek to develop historical narratives which "grant significance to the political experience of a social group" do. However, the question remains as to whether or not the above definition of political myth which is based on works concerned with the sixteenth to the nineteenth century, is still valid for the twenty-first century. The last part of the article addresses this question through an analysis of two contemporary examples namely Anders Fogh Rasmussen's narrative of the development of Danish foreign affairs in relation to Iraq in 2003 and George

W. Bush's narrative of American exceptionalism in relation to the impending war in Afghanistan in 2001.

Political Myth in the Twenty-first Century: The Freedom Fighter

During the spring and summer of 2003, Anders Fogh Rasmussen gave a number of speeches and wrote a number of articles in which he compared Saddam Hussein's current regime in Bagdad to Adolf Hitler's regime in Germany and the communist regime in the former USSR. These historical analogies were embedded in an explicit historical narrative, according to which Fogh Rasmussen's liberal/conservative coalition government, which came to power in 2001, had brought Denmark out of the shade of the Social Democrats' and Social Liberals' "policy of adaption" and into the spotlight of important military actors who were upholding democracy and human rights across the globe (Rasmussen 2003b and Rasmussen 2003a).

For example, on August 29, 2003 on the sixtieth anniversary of Denmark's break with Nazi Germany, Fogh Rasmussen gave a speech to the Danish Navy, which was also published in the center-left newspaper *Politiken* on the same day (Rasmussen 2003b). The break with Nazi Germany in 1943 had come in the aftermath of strikes and sabotage which had swept through the country in August 1943 – later dubbed The August Rebellion. On that date sixty years ago, Fogh Rasmussen said, the people had forced the political elite to terminate their collaboration with the Germans.

In the speech Fogh Rasmussen emphasized the heroic deeds of the Danish navy who on the August 29, 1943 had sunk the ships they had been unable to evacuate to Sweden. He also criticized the Danish government who had obediently taken directions from the Germans and "had collaborated at all levels from the very beginning." Not only had the Danish government followed directions, Fogh Rasmussen said. Erik Scavenius, social-liberal foreign minister from 1940–42 and prime minister from November 1942 until August 1943, had actively collaborated, and "new historical research" revealed exactly how "active" the adaption to Germany had been.

The criticism of the Danish government's collaboration with Nazi Germany between 1940 and 1943 was similar to one Fogh Rasmussen had made in a previous article published the March 26, 2003, one week after the invasion of Iraq. Here, Fogh Rasmussen indicated that the foreign policy of the social democrats and social liberals had always been characterized by adaption to the great powers of the world. This had been evident during the Second World War when Denmark had adapted to Germany; it had been evident in the early

1980s during the missile crisis when the Social Democrats backed by the left wing and the Social Liberals had refused to support NATO's positioning of nuclear missile heads in Western Europe thereby adapting to the oppressive Communist regime in the former Soviet Union. It was evident now in 2003, when they adapted to the power of terrorist regimes represented by Saddam Hussein's regime in Iraq. This adaption was evidenced by their unwillingness to sanction Danish participation in the military campaign against Iraq (Rasmussen 2003a).

In the August speech, Fogh Rasmussen admitted that adaption to the dominant powers of the world might seem sensible. For example, the Danish government's collaboration with Nazi Germany had seemed sensible because it had kept the Danish population safe from the worst harm. However, "even though one should be careful to judge the past by the standards of the present," Fogh Rasmussen said, collaborating with the Germans was foolish even from the perspective of the past: it was foolish to think that Nazi Germany would respect Danish sovereignty. In fact, Fogh Rasmussen held, "historical research" showed that even at the time, Danish officials in Washington warned the Danish government against collaboration because the final goal of the Nazi regime was the elimination of democracy itself. Though resistance might have seemed futile at the time, Fogh Rasmussen insisted that the Nazis would still be dominating Europe if everybody had succumbed to their regime. Had it not been for the brave resistance of the "freedom fighters," Denmark would have been on the "wrong side" of the fence after the war.[8]

The evil nature of the Nazi regime displayed in its will to eliminate democracy allows Fogh Rasmussen to draw his moral and political conclusion: one must take a stance for democracy and against dictatorship, and social democrats and social liberals had continuously failed to do so. That was the case in 1943 and it was the case now when democracy was threatened once again by the forces of terrorism. The Danish people, on the other hand, had found the courage to rebel against the German occupation and had brought the collaboration government to a fall. The morale of August 29, 1943 was that "if we are serious about our values, about freedom, democracy and human rights, we must be ready to actively defend them." Therefore, the battle of the

---

8 In a speech to the Mosaic Community in Copenhagen, Fogh Rasmussen made a very similar point about the relationship between the people and the government. "The people," Fogh Rasmussen said, had saved their Jewish fellow citizens and had toppled the collaboration policy of the government. The brutality of the extermination of the Jews was, according to Fogh Rasmussen, an example of how one could never be neutral when it came to a choice between "dictatorship and freedom" (Fogh Rasmussen 2003c).

freedom fighter against Nazism does not differ substantially from liberals' and conservatives' battle against communism and the battle against Saddam Hussein's oppressive dictatorship.

In his articles and speeches in 2003 Fogh Rasmussen's communication strategy was to display his government as advocates of a liberal-idealist foreign and security politics the goal of which was liberalism by imposition. According to the liberal-idealist vision, the historical process was generated by the battle between freedom and oppression and was slowly moving the world up the ladder towards the betterment of the human race. This vision of the historical process was indebted to the neoliberal globalization debates of the 1990's in which Fogh Rasmussen had also been involved. For example, in his widely debated book from 1993 *Fra Socialstat til Minimalstat (From Social State to Minimal State)*, Fogh Rasmussen argued that liberalism was a trans-historical and trans-geographical phenomenon valid at all times and in all places and was driven by the human being's natural inclination towards freedom (Fogh Rasmussen 1993). In the context in which Fogh Rasmussen was writing, freedom equaled market economy and free trade on a global scale. However, even though freedom was a natural inclination of the human being, it was continuously being thwarted, most recently (in 1993) by the oppressive power of communist regimes and by the cultural politics of the intellectual elites of social democratic welfare states, whose purpose was to transform concrete individuals into abstract citizens.[9]

The answer to this type of oppression, Fogh Rasmussen argued, was neoliberalism. According to Fogh Rasmussen, neoliberalism meant reclaiming natural rights philosophy as the true ideological roots of liberalism: the human being in its natural state was inclined towards freedom, and this natural inclination led to the foundation of natural rights, which the state was supposed to protect. These natural rights would ensure the concreteness of the individual's life against the abstraction of oppressive state regimes; and they might found a just state which acted in accordance with the concrete way of life of individuals and the communities in which they lived. The implication was that if the government-state failed to protect the individual's natural inclination towards freedom, either by making abstract citizens out of concrete individuals, or by failing to defend the way of life of the community against an external enemy, it might be invalid as a representative of the people. In

---

9 By the term cultural politics Fogh Rasmussen seems to denote a whole range of political initiatives, most significantly state support for the arts and sciences, the curriculum and teaching methods of the public school system and a whole host of political advisory boards and committees.

Fogh Rasmussen's vision of the state, then, the historical process would bring about the perfect match between the human being in its natural state and the government which administers its way of life. When that match had been achieved on a global scale, we would find ourselves at the end of history.[10]

Fogh Rasmussen's speeches and written works pivot around a number of dichotomies of which the most significant are people versus government, and present versus past. For example, the speech to the Danish Navy portrays a dichotomy between a government elite who collaborates with Nazi Germany and the people who rightfully seek to disrupt the collaboration; in *Fra Socialstat til Minimalstat* the same elite is portrayed as oppressive and arrogant leftwing intellectuals who have also dominated the government in the post-war period.[11] This elite had failed in its duty to the people insofar as it had failed to protect their naturally grounded rights and their will towards freedom. This had been the case during the Second World War, it had been the case during the Cold War and it was once again the case in The War on Terror. The freedom fighter, on the other hand, defends the biological foundation of the state itself and ensures the match between the human being pure and simple and the government: he is a soldier fighting a just battle in the name of the people. This battle might take place on two fronts: internally against a government which fails to represent the people's concrete way of life; or externally, as a soldier of the armed forces in defense of the righteous state. The freedom fighter's battle is identical to the historical process; history here signifies two things: on one hand, it signifies the cyclical recurrence of evil which must be fought; that is why Nazism is identical to communism and Islamist terrorism. On the other hand, it signifies the movement towards historical fulfilment in a neoliberal, imminent utopia with the establishment of just states, whose sovereignty is respected.

The freedom fighter is a hybrid creature: like Kantorowicz's two-bodied king, he can either represent the individual or the species; he can show the particularity of a concrete way of life or the abstraction of that way of life in the just, sovereign state. The just battle of the freedom fighter might therefore be an individual battle vis-à-vis the state as was the case during the Second World War; or it might belong to the state itself if the political state is in

---

10 In another article from July 2001, Fogh Rasmussen refers to Fukyama's promise of The End of History when western democracies would stand victorious. Unfortunately, Fogh said, the "wise man" who had suggested such a scenario had been premature; for even though liberalism had won a great victory in 1989, the world was far from liberal, and history was far from over (Fogh Rasmussen 2001).

11 Fogh Rasmussen also reiterated this criticism of the intellectual elite in his New Year's Speech in 2002 (Fogh Rasmussen 2002).

correspondence with the natural state of the human being as is the case in the War against Terror. The fight for freedom therefore invests the human being in its natural state with the insignias of belonging to the ideal, political community, and it allows the freedom fighter to safeguard the bond between ruler and ruled, either by turning against the usurpation of the people by a power-hungry elite, or by guarding the boundaries of the just state thereby protecting the natural inclination of the human being across the globe.

While the freedom fighter shows himself in the historical example insofar as he constitutes the historical process itself, he only refers to himself: when questioned, he can always turn the other face: the human being in its natural state on one hand, the just state on the other. The reason is the assumed naturalness of the human being's inclination towards freedom, which authorizes the beginning of the battle between freedom and oppression and thereby authorizes the historical example itself. The fantasy of freedom therefore ensures that the story of the freedom fighter can be abstracted from its historical concreteness and appear in different guises.

Political Myth in the Twenty-first Century: Americanism

The content of Fogh Rasmussen's political myth differs significantly from the article's second example, namely George W. Bush's. While Fogh Rasmussen's historical analogies are embedded in a somewhat empirically founded historical narrative about the development of Danish foreign affairs, Bush's analogies are embedded in a narrative about the battle between good and evil very similar to the just war rhetoric of Saint Augustine's *The City of God against the Pagans*:[12] The war against terror is part of an ongoing story about the war between good and evil. Two cities are involved in this war; one city is unjust because it fails to combat the evil of its time and guards its citizens against it. The other city protects the way of life of its citizens by resolutely responding to the "evil of our time." According to Bush, the battle of "our time," which now depends "on us," on "our nation" and "this generation" is a just battle for freedom represented by its "brightest beacon," America, and it is authorized by God, the "power greater than any of us" (Bush 2001, 58) who is "not neutral between justice and cruelty" (Bush 2001, 73).

---

12 According to Saint Augustine the just and peace loving city is the Christian Community which has been attacked by barbarians who slaughter randomly. The government of the city of Rome has failed to protect its people. According to Augustine, Rome's failure to combat the evil of the world demonstrates its injustice. The duty of the just ruler is to wage war against evil such as the barbarians' indiscriminate murder of the innocent. According to Augustine, war against evil was a just war which guards the just citizens of the City of God.

The contours of this story appeared in the immediate aftermath of the attack on the World Trade Center on September 11, 2001 in a number of speeches such as the Address to the Nation on September eleventh, the address to Congress on September twentieth and the speech to the Defense Services on October 11. In these speeches, Bush alluded to the coming war on terror and argued for the justice of the American cause. For example, in the Address to the Nation on September 11, 2001 Bush referred to the attack on the World Trade Center and Pentagon as an attack on "our way of life" and on the "very freedom" which characterized the American people. With the attack, the American people had beheld "evil, the very worst of human nature" (Bush 2001, 57). However, rather than succumbing to the forces of evil, Bush declared that the "great people" had been stirred to the defense of "a great nation," and the government had made it its number one priority to protect the citizens from further attacks. Therefore, America, which was otherwise a peace-loving nation, had to wage war in self-defense. The war would be fought in the name of justice to prevent an otherwise impending human catastrophe brought about by the evil forces of the world. Just war was, in other words, the burden which this generation had to shoulder as a final guard against the evil of our time. The government's defense of its people, Bush said, was a defense of the "justice and peace" of America; and as America had "stood down enemies before," it would once again be prepared to defend freedom and all that is good and just in our world (Bush 2001, 58).

In an address to congress nine days later Bush compared the attack on the World Trade Center to the attack on Pearl Harbor, and argued that Islamist terrorism was heir to the murderous ideologies of the twentieth century such as Nazism and fascism, which had come back to haunt our time.[13] While the present enemy and its declaration of war might warrant a military response, it was ultimately "not a military enemy." Rather, it was an enemy of "all law, all liberty, all morality and all religion" (Bush 2001, 80). Bush therefore declared that all regimes that failed to act against terrorist activities and combat the evils of our time were unjust regimes and consequently default enemies of

---

13 Bush's first reference to the Second World War was made on National Day of Prayer and remembrance when he referred to F.D. Roosevelt's speech in which he referred to "the warm courage of national unity" (Bush 2001, 60–61); the reference to Pearl Harbor (Bush 2001, 66), and his the comparison between Islamism, Nazism and fascism (Bush 2001, 69) was first made in an address to the Congress on September 20, 2001. It was reiterated in an address to the Department of Defense Service of Remembrance at the Pentagon on October 11, 2001 (Bush 2001, 80). Bush also referred made an analogy between the Nazi genocide of the European Jews and the present suffering of the victims of the attack on the World Trade Center and Pentagon in an address to the UN General Assembly on November 10, 2001 (Bush 2001, 83).

the United States. (Bush 2001, 69). Or in the Augustinian vocabulary, they represented that other city, the City of the Pagans against the City of God.

Throughout the addresses, Bush invokes a terminology which indicates that the story of the two cities in which his historical analogies are embedded functions as a political myth. For example, Bush repeatedly uses three interconnected terms, which are related to just authority on one hand and the administration of the species on the other: "the people," "the government" and finally the "I," the presidential head of state. In the addresses, the "I" serves two mediating functions. First of all, the "I" mediates between the people and the government. For example, in the Address to the Nation on September 11, the "I" commands the government to implement "our emergency plan," and the "I" assures the nation that "our government" will continue to function normally. We could also say that the "I" acts as government on one hand while bodily representing the "us" of the people on the other. Secondly, the "I" functions as the facilitator of the just sovereign authority, the "power greater than us," whose will he executes. Through the "I," the will of the just authority coincides with the will of the people, which the "I" represents.

The "I" functions in much the same manner as Fogh Rasmussen's freedom fighter: he ensures the internal unity of people and government on one hand and the justice of the state which acts externally in defense of that unity on the other; and like Fogh Rasmussen's freedom fighter, the "I" is a two-bodied creature; as head of government, he serves an internal-administrative function which ensures the everyday life of the people. As representative of the justice of state, he serves an external-political function which grants justice to the way of life of the people and safeguards its frontiers against evil. The two-bodied "I" representing both the individual "(as part of the "our") and the species (representing "a way of life") ensures the link between the just authority on one hand and the administration of the life of the species to which he belongs on the other.

In the addresses, the term "the people" is often invoked synonymously with the nation. The two terms, however, stand in an ambivalent relationship to one another. This ambivalent relation comes to the fore in The National Day of Prayer and Remembrance Service held in the National Cathedral in Washington D.C: on September 14, 2001. Here, Bush referred to the attack on the World Trade Center and the Pentagon as an act of war, which had been waged against "us," that is the people and to which we must respond; and on behalf of the nation he offered the "deepest sympathy" to the families and friends of the victims of the attack. Bush then declared that "our purpose as a nation is firm," "yet our wounds as a people are recent and unhealed" (Bush 2001, 60–61).

In these passages, the nation seems to be equivalent to a promised land in which the people will reach fulfillment once they have regained their strength and healed their wounds. The fulfillment in the nation, however, is not confined to the American people; for the war to be commenced is a "civilization's fight," and while the American people might be bearer of the nation, the Promised Land is global and open to all those who battle against evil in the name of freedom. We could also say that the nation equals a universal form of Americanism. There is an implied analogy between the American and Jewish nation in Bush's rhetoric: the American nation is heir to the promised land; and like the Jews had suffered and fallen victim to the evil of Nazism, the American people now suffer because they have fallen victim to the evil of our own time. While Bush never mentions the Jews in the three addresses discussed above, the reference is evident elsewhere, for example in his address to the United Nations General Assembly on November 10 (Bush 2001, 83). In this address, Bush used the suffering of the European Jews to frame the suffering of September eleventh and thereby suggested that the United Nations' should support the War on Terror insofar as it was founded to prevent crimes of evil like the genocide against the European Jews (Reinbold 2011). The implication was that the Americans like the Jews are the chosen people; they are singled out by the suffering they have to endure. Thus, Bush's historical narrative which is used to justify the War on Terror is a story of the exodus of God's chosen people, who must deliver the world form evil. The two-bodied "I" representing the individual as well as the species speaks on behalf of the nation and thereby comes to incorporate it. Bush's myth is therefore double layered: on one hand, it is a semi-religious myth of an exodus, on the other it is the myth of the liberal state in which the head of state balances between people and government.

Fogh Rasmussen's liberal myth of the freedom fighter differs significantly from what we might refer to as Bush's semi-religious myth of Americanism. Nevertheless, they serve similar functions: they justify the justice of the state at war by referring it to a highest good and an ultimate authority. This authority is grounded in a natural state in which the human being lives in accordance with his or her nature. The fantasy of the sovereign, Fogh Rasmussen's freedom fighter or Bush's Americanism, mediates between the human being in its natural state and the human subject invested with the insignias of belonging to a political community. The sovereign, however, has no reference: it ensures that the political myth can show either side of the coin: the natural order of the human being or the abstraction of that order in the state.

Towards a Theory of Political Myth

This article has addressed the use of historical analogies and historical narratives in the justification of Western warfare in the twenty-first century within the context of political myth. The article suggested that previous conceptualizations of political myth revolved around two problems: the legitimacy of government and the assumed naturalness of myth as a cognitive function. The question was therefore raised as to 1) the relationship between myth as a cognitive category which is always already there, and the political myth which legitimizes the rule of state or state-like groups, and 2) the relationship between myth as a natural part of the human body and myth as a narrative discernible in the historical analogies and historical narratives used in the justification of warfare.

The article suggested that this question had been addressed previously by Kantorowicz and Arendt in different, historical contexts. However, the analysis of two contemporary examples showed that while the content of Fogh Rasmussen's and Bush's myths differ from the myth of the King's two bodies and the myth of the nation, they still operate within the same framework: they are organized around a fantasy of the sovereign which mediates between the human being in its natural state and the political subject. Thus, the legal myth of the King's two bodies, the myth of the nation, the historical narrative of the freedom fighter and the story of the exodus from evil all inscribe a relationship between the ruler and his or her source of authority. This relationship is sanctioned by the natural state of the human being itself towards which the just ruler will strive.

The biological foundation of myth is therefore related to the nature of the human being itself, stripped of all its political endowments and reduced to its animal state. Whether the natural state is the state of the heavenly Kingdom, the nation state, the state of individual freedom or Americanism, in striving towards the natural state the ruler ensures his or her legitimacy in administering the earth and in protecting it from the outside. Myth has a dual nature, then. On one hand, it refers to a beginning, an originary state of nature towards which the human being is naturally drawn. On the other hand, it refers to a narrative which grants significance to the political experience of a social group, as Bottici would have it. The dual nature of myth, however, relies on a fantasy of the sovereign which organizes the two sides of the political myth and ensures that they can appear in many different guises. Political myth, then, might neither be a founding narrative, nor a cognitive function through which we process the world. Rather, it might be what makes us repeat the initial jointure between the individual and the species. Perhaps it is the case, then, that the supposed biological function of myth on one hand and the legitimation of "sovereign" rule on the other reflects a split between the animal and the human internal to the human being itself. This would render political myth a narrative of the emergence of human subjectivity rather than a narrative of the glory of the state.

References

Angstrom, Jan. 2011. "Mapping the Competing Historical Analogies of the War on Terrorism: The Bush Presidency." *International Relations* 24: 224–42.

Anderson, Benedict. 2006. *Imagined Communities: Reflections on the Origin and Spread of Nationalism*. London: Verso.

Arendt, Hannah. 1994. *The Origins of Totalitarianism*. New York: Harcourt Inc.

Augustine. 2003. *Concerning the City of God against the Pagans*. Translated by Henry Bettenson. London: Penguin.

Blair, Tony. 2001. "Speech at the Labour Party Conference." *The Guardian*, October 2. Accessed September 20, 2015. http://www.theguardian.com/politics/2001/oct/02/labourconference.labour6.

Blumenberg, Hans. 1985. *Work on Myth*. Translated by Robert M. Wallace. Cambridge, Massachusetts: MIT Press.

Bottici, Chiara. 2007. *A Philosophy of Political Myth*. Cambridge: Cambridge University Press.

Bottici, Chiara, and Benoit Challand. 2010. *The Myth of the Clash of Civilization*. New York: Routledge.

Bush, George W. 2001. *Selected Speeches of George W. Bush*. Accessed September 20, 2015. http://georgewbush-whitehouse.archives.gov/infocus/bushrecord/documents/Selected_Speeches_George_W_Bush.pdf

Campana, Aurélie. 2009. "Collective Memory and Violence: The Use of Myths in the Chechen Separatist Ideology, 1991–1994." *Journal of Muslim Minority Affairs* 29: 43–56.

———. 1972. *The Philosophy of Symbolic Forms: Mythical Thought*. Translated by Ralph Manheim. New Haven: Yale University Press.

Duara, Prasenjit. 1995. *Rescuing History from the Nation: Questioning Narratives of Modern China*. Chicago: University of Chicago Press.

Espiritu, Yen Le, and Diana Wolf. 2013. "The Appropriation of American War Memories: A Critical Juxtaposition of the Holocaust and the Vietnam War." *Social Identities* 19: 188–203.

Esch, Joanne. 2010. "Legitimizing 'The War on Terror': Political Myth in Official-Level Rhetoric." *Political Psychology*: 357–91.

Foucault, Michel. 1998. *The History of Sexuality Vol. 1: The Will to Knowledge*. Translated by Robert Hurley. New York: Penguin.

———. 2008. *The Birth of Biopolitics: Lectures at the College de France 1978–79*. Translated by Graham Burchell. Basingstoke: Palgrave.

Hobsbawm, Eric, and Terence Ranger, eds. 2012. *The Invention of Tradition*. Cambridge: Cambridge University Press.

Jordan, William C. 1997. "Preface." In *The King's Two Bodies: A Study in Medieval Political Theology*, by Ernst Kantorowicz, ix–xv. Princeton: Princeton University Press.

Kant, Immanuel. 2000. *Critique of the Power of Judgment*. Translated by Paul Guyer. Cambridge: Cambridge University Press.

Kantorowicz, Ernst H. 1997. *The King's Two Bodies: A Study in Medieval Political Theology*. Princeton: Princeton University Press.

Rasmussen, Anders F. 1993. *Fra Socialstat til Minimalstat*. Copenhagen: Samleren.

———. 2001. "En global pagt." *Erhverstidende*, July 3.

———.2002."Nytårstale."AccessedSeptember20,2015.http://statsministeriet. videoportal.digizuite.dk/default.aspx?ReturnUrl=%2f#mainpage/73/_/ false.

———. 2003a. "Hvad kan det nytte?" *Berlingske Tidende*. March 26.

———. 2003b. "60 år efter: Samarbejdspolitikken var moralsk svigt." *Politiken*, August 29.

———. 2003c. "Det danske lys I det nazistiske mørke." *Kristeligt Dagblad*, October 10.

Reinbold, Jenna. 2011. "Political Myth and the Sacred Center of Human Rights: The Universal Declaration and the Narrative of "Inherent Human Dignity." *Human Rights Review* 12: 147–71.

Santner, Eric. 2011. *The Royal Remains: The People's Two Bodies and the Endgames of Sovereignty*. Chicago: University of Chicago Press.

Schmitt, Carl. 2005. *Political Theology: Four Chapters on the Concept of Sovereignty*. Translated by George Schwab. Chicago: University of Chicago Press.

Measuring Identity
Critique and the Notions of Truth and Violence
in Judith Butler's *Gender Trouble*

Johanna Sjöstedt [1]

Abstract

2015 marks the twenty-fifth year since the publication of the American philosopher Judith Butler's contemporary classic *Gender Trouble: Feminism and the Subversion of Identity*. In this article, I discuss Butler's notions of truth and violence in relation to identity against the backdrop of an account of developments in critical philosophy, with particular focus on the thought of nineteenth-century German philosophers Georg W. F. Hegel and Friedrich Nietzsche. Using the French film *Tomboy*, which tells the story of a young girl who decides to appear as boy, as a case in point, I show the importance of addressing the question of the relationship between the concepts of truth, gender identity, and pain. In the first part of the article, I contrast the notion of truth and the distinction between appearance and reality in the thought of Hegel to the thought of Nietzsche. Through a comparison between Nietzsche and Butler, I then show that Butler follows in Nietzsche's footsteps in the deconstruction of the distinction between appearance and reality in her understanding of gender identity. However, I argue that Butler's thought harbors internal tensions regarding what principle should be substituted for truth in feminist critique. Focusing on ambiguities in the concept of violence, I also show that Butler on the one hand uses violence as a way to condemn oppression in the domain of gender identity but on the other hand considers violence to be constitutive of the subject. Thus violence appears to be at once unavoidable and morally reprehensible.

---

1 Johanna Sjöstedt recently received her MA in the history of ideas from the Department of Literature, the History of Ideas, and Religion at the University of Gothenburg.

> The truth shall make you free.
> –John 8:32

> How is it established for all the
> world that true judgments give
> more enjoyment than false
> ones?
> –Nietzsche, *The Antichrist*

A few years ago, the French film *Tomboy* premiered in cinemas across Europe (Sciamma 2011). Set during the summer holidays, the film portrays the young Laure and her little sister when they have just moved to a rather dilapidated area somewhere in France with their parents. Encountering the children in the yard, the androgynous Laure decides to appear as a boy and calls herself Michaël. Watching the film, the spectator follows her in scenes where her passing as a boy is successful, yet we witness her fear of getting caught. When she defends her little sister from bullying, leaving a bruise on the face of another boy, her parents discovered what she had done and forced her to reveal her gender to her new friends, among them Lisa, who earlier in the film softly kissed her on the cheek. In the last scene the two children meet again. "What's your name?" Lisa asks, receiving a simple "Laure" for a reply. This is the concluding line of the film.

Using this film as an example, what insights can be gained in the domain of feminist critique? If we consider the reasons for the behavior of the parents, we find that they frame the question of gender in terms of truth. In a heartbreaking scene, Laure's mother claims that she does not mind her daughter's desire to appear as a boy, but adds that the game cannot last. What will happen when Laure starts school in the fall? Moreover, she has lied to her friends; now she must tell the *truth*. Although the film shows the violence implicit in the mother's demand, the parents are by no means portrayed as cruel and overall the relationship between children and parents is described in warm colors. Those who force Laure to reveal the truth of her gender to her friends are not evil. Nonetheless, it is clear that they inflict pain. According to American anthropologist Talal Asad, the Western tradition is steeped in the notion that truth and freedom are intertwined, epitomized perhaps most clearly in John's formulation that "the truth shall make you free" (Asad 2009, 39). Against the backdrop of the film, we are nonetheless faced with a different situation where the question of the truth

of Laure's gender neither brings freedom nor salvation, but rather constitutes a form of violence that inflicts pain. Perhaps we could even be tempted
into formulating a different saying: "the truth shall make you suffer." But
then we have to ask ourselves what truth is. We also have to ask what it would
mean to raise the question of gender identity, its relationship to truth and
the notion of pain.

Critique between Dialectics and Genealogy

The historical question of how sex became the subject of a discourse of truth,
thereby introducing the possibility of lying in the domain of gender identity,
is the major theme in French philosopher and historian Michel Foucault's
The Will to Knowledge: The History of Sexuality, Volume 1 (Foucault 1998). In this
essay I will focus on the philosophical roots of the question of the place of
truth or reality in critique through a reading of nineteenth-century German
philosophers G. W. F. Hegel and Friedrich Nietzsche. Their works have served
as points of departure for several intellectual strands of the twentieth century
that are read in the humanities today, including neo-Marxism, the Frankfurt
School, existentialism, deconstruction and genealogy. Another way to put it
is that twentieth-century thinkers in various ways struggle with the legacy of
Hegel, confronted on the one hand by the effects of political projects inspired
by left-Hegelianism, and by the philosophical criticism of Nietzsche and his
genealogical successors on the other. Contrasting the notion of truth and the
distinction between appearance and reality in the thought of Hegel and critique inspired by him to the thought of Nietzsche in the first part of the essay,
I will in the second part move on to the problem of identity in feminism in
general, and in the early thought of well-known American philosopher Judith
Butler in particular. I will focus on *Gender Trouble: Feminism and the Subversion
of Identity*, Butler's first major work that became a contemporary classic and
propelled her to academic stardom (Butler 1999a). 2015 marks twenty-five
years since its publication and my essay could be read as a modest attempt to
pay tribute to her work. By reading Butler against the backdrop of Hegel and
Nietzsche, rather than more obvious references such as Freud and Foucault, I
hope to shed new light on her philosophy and to formulate questions worthy
of further consideration, both in relation to the development in Butler's later
work and in feminist theory more generally speaking.

"Critique" stems from the ancient Greek words *kríno* and *kritikós*, which
means to sift, discern, perceive, and judge (Ritter and Gründer 1976, 1249).
Critique appears in Plato's dialogue "Theaetetus," where Socrates's methodo-

logical midwifery is described as "examining whether the thought which the mind of the young man brings forth is a false idol or a noble and true birth" (Plato 2015). During the Enlightenment, critique became an important concern for philosophy and society as a whole. With his three major works on critique published 1780–1790, German philosopher Immanuel Kant transformed modern philosophy into an essentially critical project, the effects of which still resonate throughout the twenty-first century (Adorno 1998, 281). What distinguished Kantian critique was the principle of immanence. The critique of reason was to be undertaken in the name of reason itself and pure it of its false pretentions (Kant 1998, 100). Another important aspect of Kant's philosophy was that it placed subjectivity at the center of philosophy, conceptualizing human perception of the world as dependent on the constitution of the subject as such.

If Kant thought of the subject as universal, Hegel introduced the problem of perspectivism into modern philosophy; the possibility that different subjects have different perceptions or perspectives of reality that are in conflict. Temporalizing critical reason, Hegel conceived of history as the unfolding of reason's dialectical movement, where the different perspectives are played out against each other, continuously yielding higher forms yet preserving the previous perspectives within the new ones. According to Hegel, the task of philosophy is to "eliminate the contingent" (Hegel 1975, 28). Reason is defined as the critical faculty that through the multifarious impressions that meet the senses has the ability to discern the immanent order of reason, in the end to comprise the point of view of world history itself, which is described as "the sum total of all possible perspectives" (Hegel 1975, 30). These notions of reason, history, and critique are also imported into the Marxist critique of ideology and the Frankfurt school (Honneth 2009). In the words of American political philosopher Wendy Brown, Marx's concept of critique is founded upon the notion that the critic could and ought to have insight into the reality behind the shifting nature of the world as it appears to the senses. "Critique," she writes, "is premised upon a historically necessary mystification of reality … and it promises to scientifically decode that mystification" (Brown 2009, 12). Another important aspect of this form of critique is the concept of ideology, which is also closely intertwined with the notion of false consciousness. Ideology is that which distorts reality and hides a truth that only the critic could reveal. Critique is thus construed as the revelation of truth, a revelation that is completed in the revolutionary act that changes the historical conditions that gave rise to the false consciousness.

Nietzsche's thought could in many ways be read as a revolt against this notion of history, which was not only formulated in the philosophy of Hegel but rather defined nineteenth-century Germany as a whole (Persson 2007). In his short essay "On Truth and Lying in the Extra Moral Sense," Nietzsche rejects Hegel's idealistic claim that the relationship between subject and object could be framed in terms of reason and grasped through conceptual knowledge, stressing that these are two separate realms where there can be no translation. According to Nietzsche, the relation rather consists of an "aesthetic stance" that requires a "freely fictionalizing and freely inventive middle sphere" that is human imagination (Nietzsche 1989, 252). Hegel's notion of "the sum total of all possible perspectives" is replaced with a constitutive perspectivism considered to be the "fundamental condition of all life" (Nietzsche 1998a, 4). Nietzsche rejects the idea of the sublation of different perspectives into one singular point of view, since this "could be decided only by the criterion of the *right perception*, i.e. by a standard *which does not exist*" (Nietzsche 1989, 252). In Nietzsche's view, it is precisely the specific perspective of the living individual that constitutes the condition for evaluation at all, and the perspective that could unite the perspectives of different individuals would entail the end of critical judgment as such. According to Nietzsche, there is "only a seeing from a perspective, only a 'knowing' from a perspective" (Nietzsche 1918, 124).

Nietzsche's philosophy is also a fundamental attack on any notion of transcendence, the belief that there is a more true reality behind or beyond the sensible experience of the world. The idea of an existence in another realm, whether it is formulated in Plato's concept of forms or in the Christian dream of an afterlife, Nietzsche considers to be a symptom of an all too human desire to find stable points of reference in a world that is inherently chaotic (Nietzsche 1989). Nietzsche thus undertakes a radical deconstruction of the dichotomy between appearance and reality. In *Twilight of the Idols*, he writes, "with the real world we have also done away with the apparent one!" (Nietzsche 1998b, 20). Recalling that the task of philosophy according to Hegel was to eliminate the contingent and to discern, behind the disorder of the world as it appeared to the senses, the underlying structure of reason, we see that Nietzsche not only departs from the idea of a standard that unifies the separate perspectives into one, but that he also rejects the existence of a supersensible point of reference in whose name the falseness of the given world could be measured. This also entails a major shift in comparison to the notion of critique developed by Hegel, left-Hegelianism and the Frankfurt

School, for whom the distinction between appearance and reality played a decisive role.

It should be stressed that both Hegel and Nietzsche express different versions of immanent critique, in the sense that their respective critical projects proceed by way of a standard that is external neither with respect to the object that is being measured, nor with respect to the subject who performs the measuring. However, because of the ambiguous status of reason within Hegel's thought, where reason is immanent in the world and also the driving force behind the course of history, we end up with a notion of immanent critique that is undertaken in the name of a principle that tends to assume a transcendent status. By way of an all-including immanence, underpinned by the notion of historical progress, the concepts of reason and history intertwined are elevated into a transcendent standard for critique.

In Nietzsche, on the other hand, the category of life is substituted for the concepts of reason, history, and truth with respect to judgment. As was shown previously, he rejects the possibility of an objective point of reference from which the falseness of the given world could be measured. This does not entail the end of critical judgment, but rather calls for an affirmation of perspectivism. Critique, according to Nietzsche, ought not to appeal to truth or reason, but should rather be undertaken in the name of life:

> The falseness of an opinion is not for us any objection to it: it is here, perhaps, that our new language sounds most strangely. The question is how far an opinion is life furthering, life preserving. (Nietzsche 1998a, 4)

Life, not truth, becomes the standard for a Nietzschean critique. Moreover, this also means that the category of truth is displaced within Nietzsche's thought. If the notions of truth, freedom and pleasure are intermingled in the Western tradition, Nietzschean critique becomes a space where this conjunction is disentangled. In other words, truth is no longer analytically intertwined with freedom; the thought of a truth that inflicts pain no longer an oxymoron.

Feminism and the Question of Identity

The concept of truth and the interrelated distinction between appearance and reality also constitute major issues in feminist theory, with respect to the question of the status of gender and sexual identity and gender performance in feminism. In her classic article "Compulsory Heterosexuality and Lesbian

Existence," first published in 1980, the American poet Adrienne Rich develops a critique of the invisibility of lesbian life both within the feminist movement and in society in general. Rich's critique starts from the notion that the oppression of lesbians is constituted by the obliteration of lesbian identity as such. According to Rich, lesbianism is a transhistorical and transcultural phenomenon and against the backdrop of a heterosexist society that persistently disavows this lesbianism, she proclaims the affirmation of lesbian identity to be a productive political strategy:

> For lesbian existence to realize its political content in an ultimately liberating form, the erotic choice must deepen and expand into conscious woman identification – into lesbian feminism. (Rich 1993, 245)

The thought of Rich represents a second wave version of feminism, which was subjected to criticism by poststructuralist feminists in the 1990's. Working in the wake of Hegel and Nietzsche's criticism of the great systematic philosopher, Judith Butler is one of the most prominent thinkers of this period. Her dissertation in philosophy discussed the notion of desire in Hegel's *Phenomenology of Spirit* and her thought continues to be deeply informed by Hegel (Butler 1999b). Yet her texts are also marked by distinctively Nietzschean tendencies.

In *Gender Trouble* Butler claims that the question of the subject is "crucial" for feminist politics and undertakes a thorough critique of the assumptions about women's identity and the political subject of women that permeate feminism (Butler 1999a, 5). The political is located in "the very signifying practices that establish regulate, and deregulate identity" (Butler 1999a, 188). Rather than considering oppression to consist in the exclusion of a particular identity from cultural representation or political congregations, she thus suggests that oppression is located in the standard that establishes the subject as such:

> The domains of political and linguistic 'representation' set out in advance the criterion by which subjects themselves are formed, with the result that representation is extended only to what can be acknowledged as a subject. (Butler 1999a, 4)

In other words, according to Butler there is no subject that precedes the political practice that seeks liberation in the name of a specific category of identity;

moreover, the tools by which liberation is attempted in themselves establish new limits and criteria of what is to be counted as a subject, a process with potentially oppressive effects. Thus the kernel of Butler's political project lies not in the affirmation of a particular identity, but rather in the denaturalization of identity as such, which exposes the contingency of identity and thereby contributes to a broadening of the cultural field for the expression of gender and sexuality.

In analogy to Nietzsche, who objected to the Hegelian notion of an all-including perspective, Butler rejects the possibility of a final standard against which the true nature of identity could be measured:

> [If] there is no preexisting identity by which an act or attribute might be measured; there would be no true or false, real or distorted acts of gender, and the postulation of a true gender identity would be revealed as a regulatory fiction. ... Gender can be neither true nor false, neither real nor apparent, neither original nor derived. (Butler 1999a, 180)

In this quote, we also find a Nietzschean dimension with respect to the critique of the distinction between appearance and reality, where Butler explicitly rejects the notion of a "true" identity. Rather than finding a natural woman behind the layers of patriarchal misrepresentation of women, it is precisely the notion of truth in the domain of gender that ought to be criticized. For Butler, the postulate of a natural woman is to be considered an effect of power that should be subjected to critical interrogation.

Butler also follows Nietzsche with respect to his rejection of the Hegelian claim that the bond between subject and object should be framed in terms of knowledge, and argues that feminism should move from an epistemological concept of identity to one of meaning (Butler 1999a, 184). Like Nietzsche, she also conceives of a radical immanence with no objective point of reference beyond the realm of meaning from which a judgment of identity could proceed. It is only "*within* the practices of repetitive signifying that a subversion of identity becomes possible" (Butler 1999a, 185). At this point, however, we are faced with a delicate problem. If there is no viable standard for the measurement of identity and all attempts to establish such a standard is deemed to be an effect of power, then by what standard ought feminist critique proceed? By what standard should we make judgments about the constellations of gendered acts that might effectuate the subversion of identity that Butler proclaims as a political strategy? How to evaluate different identities?

In *Sacrificial Logics: Feminism and the Critique of Identity*, the Canadian philosopher Allison Weir discusses this aspect of Butler's thought. What Butler lacks, according to Weir, are

> normative criteria for distinguishing acceptable from unacceptable forms of identity. This is a crucial distinction, because without it, it becomes impossible to grant the importance of affirming *political* identities, and identifications, without lapsing into paradox. (Weir 1996, 128)

In the preface to the second edition of *Gender Trouble*, Butler addresses this kind of criticism. She claims that the subversion of identity depends on context, which means there can be no universal rules for when the exposure of the contingent nature of identity gives rise to a change in gendered norms, or when it only means a further entrenchment of those norms. Moreover, she declares herself to be uninterested in developing standards in order to judge between the subversive and the non-subversive: "the effort to name the criterion for subversiveness will always fail, and ought to" (Butler 1999a, xxi). Another reason for Butler's hesitation is that she suspects that this kind of judgment might become part of the very regime of oppression that she criticizes. She writes that she in *Gender Trouble*

> sought to undermine any and all efforts to wield a discourse of truth to delegitimize minority gendered and sexual practices. This doesn't mean that all minority practices ought to be condoned or celebrated, but it does mean that we ought to be able to think them before we come to any kinds of conclusions about them. (Butler 1999a, viii)

Measuring identity in any form therefore proves to be a dicey enterprise; it means running the risk of enforcing a new order of oppression. Therefore, Butler considers the task of feminism to be the critical interrogation of the grids of intelligibility that regulate the appearance of identity as such, rather than developing criteria in order to judge between different identities.

However, Butler's thought also harbors internal tensions, in particular concerning her understanding of identity and its connection the concept of violence. On the one hand, the idea that the politics of identity constitutes a kind of violence functions as the normative foundation of her criticism of feminism and society in general with respect to the identities that are disavowed as unreal. In other words, she appeals to the notion of violence as something

inherently bad. However, at the same time she claims that violence is constitutive of the formation of the subject as such, which means that violence in
some ways proves to be unavoidable. Although Butler doesn't propose her
own theory of the subject in *Gender Trouble*, this is evident in her later work,
where she speaks of an "originary violence," and claims that subjection is "the
condition of becoming a subject" (Butler 1997, 25, 7). In *Gender Trouble*, she
sometimes speaks of violence in terms of more or less violence, thereby introducing a standard to measure between different formations of identity. This
occurs in a context where she discusses how the subversion of the gendered
categories that we ordinarily take for granted introduces an opening for a
radical re-evaluation of identities, which may lead to the realization that "the
sedimented, and reified field of gender 'reality' is understood as one that
might be made differently and, indeed, *less violently*" (Butler 1999a, xxiii, ital-
ics added). Thus there is an ambivalence in the concept of violence as it is
used by Butler; it sometimes functions as a norm in order to condemn the
violence of excluding some people from representation in culture or politics, and it is sometimes thought of as being unavoidable, rather connoting a
notion of difference in degree.

The tensions in Butler's work compel new questions. Should feminist philosophy accept the quantitative measure of the *amount* of violence as a productive standard of critique? Or would it be more productive to consider a different notion of violence and rather speak of various qualities of violence, more
or less life-affirming kinds of violence, to hark back to Nietzsche? Returning
to the film *Tomboy* discussed in the introduction to this essay, it was evident
that truth in relation to gender inflicted pain.[2] Could pain be understood as
a correlate to violence? How should the relationship between gender identity,
violence, and pain be conceptualized in the field of feminist critique?

Coda

Using the film *Tomboy* as my point of departure, I began this essay by questioning the Western assumption of an association between truth and freedom.
I also advanced the hypothesis that, on some occasions, truth might inflict

---

2 It has been suggest that a consequence of Butler's appropriation of psychoanalysis is that there
would be a difference between the idea that the unconscious is violated and the phenomenological
experience of pain. However, it seems to me that Butler rather takes advantage of the rhetorical
effects of the ambiguity of the concept of violence that I point out here, using it to produce a powerful
critique of oppression through appealing to the readers' own experiences of pain in the domains of
gender identity and sexuality. I would thus argue that the experience of pain is tacitly presupposed
throughout much of Butler's work, including *Gender Trouble*.

pain. Tracing the question of truth and the distinction between appearance and reality to its historical roots, focusing on the thought of nineteenth-century German philosophers Hegel and Nietzsche, I showed implications of this association for feminist theory. In a move similar to that employed by Nietzsche, Butler deconstructed the notion of truth in the domain of identity and rejected the idea of a "true" identity in whose name the falseness of the gendered appearances that we experience in everyday life could be measured. While Nietzsche substituted the notion of life for that of truth with respect to critical judgment, it was however unclear how Butler envisioned the principle by which feminist critique should proceed. She left the reader with unresolved tensions and underdeveloped concepts concerning violence and pain in connection to the question of identity.[3] However, to explicate and further investigate the themes and questions raised here remains beyond the scope of this essay. I hope the very formulation of them has a value of its own.

---

3 Butler herself would return to this problem in her subsequent work *Bodies that Matter*, through a critical engagement with Freud's notion of narcissism (Butler 1993).

References

Adorno, Theodor W. 1998. *Critical Models: Interventions and Catchwords.* Translated by Henry W. Pickford. New York. Columbia University Press.

Asad, Talal. 2009. "Free Speech, Blasphemy, and Secular Criticism." In *Is Critique Secular? Blasphemy, Injury and Free Speech,* edited by Talal Asad, Wendy Brown, Judith Butler, and Saba Mahmood, 14–57. Berkeley: University of California Press.

Brown, Wendy. 2009. "Introduction." In *Is Critique Secular? Blasphemy, Injury and Free Speech,* edited by Talal Asad, Wendy Brown, Judith Butler, and Saba Mahmood, 1–13. Berkeley: University of California Press.

Butler, Judith. 1993. *Bodies That Matter: On the Discursive Limits of Sex.* New York: Routledge.

———. 1997. *The Psychic Life of Power: Theories in Subjection.* Stanford: Stanford University Press 1997.

———. 1999a. *Gender Trouble: Feminism and the Subversion of Identity.* New York: Routledge.

———. 1999b. *Subjects of Desire: Hegelian Reflections in Twentieth Century France.* New York: Columbia University Press.

Foucault, Michel. 1998. *The Will to Knowledge: The History of Sexuality, Volume 1.* Translated by Robert Hurley. London: Penguin.

Hegel, Georg W. F. 1975. *Lectures on the Philosophy of World History.* Translated by H. B. Nesbit. Cambridge: Cambridge University Press.

Historisches Wörterbuch der Philosophie Volume IV. 1976. Edited by Joachim Ritter and Karlfried Gründer. Basel and Stuttgart: Schwabe & Co.

Honneth, Axel. 2009. *Pathologies of Reason: On the Legacy of Critical Theory.* Translated by. James Ingram. New York: Columbia University.

Kant, Immanuel. 1998. *Critique of Pure Reason.* Edited by Paul Guyer and Allen W. Wood. Cambridge: Cambridge University Press.

Nietzsche, Friedrich. 1918. *The Genealogy of Morals.* Translated by Horace B. Samuel. New York: Boni and Liveright.

———. 1989. "On Truth and Lying in the Extra Moral Sense." In *Friedrich Nietzsche on Rhetoric and Language,* edited by Sander L. Gilman, Carole Blair, and David J. Parent, 246–57. New York: Oxford University Press.

———. 1998a. *Beyond Good and Evil.* Translated by Marion Faber. Oxford: Oxford University Press.

———. 1998b. *Twilight of the Idols.* Translated by Duncan Large. Oxford: Oxford University Press.

Persson, Mats. 2007. "Nietzsche och revolten mot historien." *Lychnos* 45: 95–128.

Plato 2015. "Theaetetus." Translated by Benjamin Jowett. http://classics.mit. edu/Plato/theatu.html (accessed September 25, 2015).

Rich, Adrienne. 1993. "Compulsory Heterosexuality and Lesbian Existence." In *The Lesbian and Gay Studies Reader,* edited by Henry Abelove, Michèle Aina Barale, and David M. Halperin, 227–54. New York: Routledge.

Sciamma, Céline. 2011. *Tomboy.*

Weir, Allison. 1996. *Sacrificial Logics: Feminist Theory and the Critique of Identity.* New York: Routledge.

"Gone to Earth" 1975

Sexuality and Ideology in the Last Words of Per Wahlöö

Per Hellgren

Abstract

When the Swedish crime writer Per Wahlöö died in 1975 he and his writing part-
ner, Maj Sjöwall, had barely managed to finish their final novel, *The Terrorists*
(1975). Following the recent discovery of Wahlöö's last notes from his deathbed,
previously unknown to the public, the author explores Wahlöö's plans for an 11th
Martin Beck novel, and how these plans fit into the ideological legacy of Sjöwall-
Wahlöö.

Introduction

When *The Terrorists*, the final novel of Swedish crime writers Per Wahlöö and
Maj Sjöwall, was released in the autumn of 1975, Wahlöö had already died
and the crime saga featuring Martin Beck was over. Per Wahlöö's last words
on paper, recently discovered in Sweden, reveal the planning of a new, eleventh, novel in the series. This article explores those final words from Wahlöö
and their relation to the overall Sjöwall-Wahlöö corpus. More specifically, it
analyzes the relationship between Wahlöö's notes, the sexual politics of the
series, and the critique of the Swedish welfare state.

This article is divided into two main sections. The first addresses the question of female sexuality as freedom and a means of revolution. The second
discusses the view on ideology running through the Beck series.

My aim with this article is, through the study of Wahlöö's last words, to
make a constribution to the research concerning the roots of ideology –
sexual and political – in the modern wave of crime fiction, also known as
Scandinavian Noir, Nordic Noir or Swedish Crime. Several modern Swedish crime writers, such as Henning Mankell and Stieg Larsson, depict a view
of Sweden which stems from the leftist political environment in the Swedish
1970s, in which Sjöwall-Wahlöö became the very first bestselling phenomenon with their political crime fiction novels. This world of ideas also exists,
to some extent, in Per Wahlöö's own early works written between 1961 and
'68. Therefore I explore the entire legacy as one corpus (years 1961–1975),
an approach that has not been taken before. In particular, my own theory of

Wahlöö's female characters as metaphors for individual freedom and sexual revolution is a new contribution to Sjöwall-Wahlöö research (Hellgren 2015, 190–94, 212–14).

In this paper, I will ask how the sexuality in Sjöwall-Wahlöö responds to the "last words" of Per Wahlöö. I am also interested in what ideologies lay behind Wahlöö's female characters, how this conception of women and their sexuality change and manifests itself in the Sjöwall-Wahlöö corpus and how the notion of the oppressive welfare state in Sjöwall-Wahlöö return in the "last words" of Wahlöö. Finally, I am interested in which Marxist conception of ideology is presented by Sjöwall-Wahlöö and what impact the structure of the welfare state have on the individuals in the novels and works in question.

Sjöwall & Wahlöö

Between the years 1965 and 1975, Per Wahlöö, together with his companion and fiancée, Maj Sjöwall, wrote ten genre-challenging novels in their Martin Beck Crime Mystery Series, also known as "Novel of a Crime." Today, all of them are widely considered classics of the genre, translated into forty languages and selling in the millions. And still – fifty years after the first novel *Roseanna* was released in 1965 – Japanese and German tourists wander about the streets of Stockholm searching for the office of Inspector Beck.

Crime writers Per Wahlöö (1926–1975) and Maj Sjöwall (1935–) met in the summer of 1962 when Wahlöö was working on the weekly journal *Folket i Bild* and Maj Sjöwall was employed as art director on the magazine *Idun*, both situated in the same building in Stockholm. Their professional relationship began in secrecy when Sjöwall transcribed and rewrote the novel *The Assignment* (Uppdraget) in 1963 for Wahlöö. A personal relationship developed soon afterwards. After another two individually-authored novels, Wahlöö started to write the Beck series together with Sjöwall in 1965, which resulted in their first joint publication, *Roseanna*. In this gruesome murder mystery, that shook the very foundations of the Nordic crime fiction market, Martin Beck appeared for the first time when he and his colleagues investigate a brutal murder of an American woman found in the water of a popular tourist canal.

John-Henri Holmberg (2014) argues that *Roseanna* was not an immediate success in Sweden. The critics found it too gritty, too depressive, too dark, and too brutal. Gradually, however, Sjöwall-Wahlöö's novels became a literary bestselling phenomenon. Holmberg identifies the breakthrough of the hard-boiled style in Swedish crime during the 1960s as a phenomenon in which younger generations – grown up on hard-boiled crime novels published in cheap paperback editions, rather than the bourgeois Agatha Christie mysteries of their parents – fully enjoyed the social criticism in the American style (Holmberg 2014, 10–11).

Between 1966 and 1975, a further nine Beck novels appeared. Their novel *Den skrattande polisen* (The Laughing Policeman, 1968) won an Edgar Allan Poe Award in 1971, garnering them an international reputation and following. With the Beck-novels an interest for Swedish crime appeared all over the world (Sjöwall, personal interview August 20, 2012). Most recently, interest has centered upon Stieg Larsson (1954–2004) and his three Swedish noir novels featuring Lisbeth Salander.

In the 1960s, crime was seen as a social problem, not as a private aberration, nor a monster against the normality of the rest of society, as it had been in the earlier crime fiction in Sweden from writers like Maria Lang and H-K Rönblom (Wendelius 1999, 51). Therefore the link to sociology, psychology and philosophy in the crime novels of Sjöwall-Wahlöö is more explicit than in earlier works of Swedish crime.

In his preface to *Roseanna*, Swedish crime writer Henning Mankell identifies the element of social criticism as the defining feature of Sjöwall-Wahlöö's writing: "They wanted to use the crime and the crime investigation as a mirror of Swedish society – later also of the world around us... They had realized the big unexplored area of letting crime fiction be the frame of social-critical stories" (Mankell 2012, 6–7). This defining feature also appears in Wahlöö's final words (entitled "Gone to Earth").

Swedish film scholar Michael Tapper (2014) argues that the Beck series moves from bearing the imprint of Sigmund Freud (in the early novels) to Karl Marx (in the latter ones). This means that the ten novels of the series function as a critical bridge that begins with the notion of crime as sexually conditioned and concludes with Herbert Marcuse's repressive welfare state in which sexual liberation is a deceitful facade for hiding sexuality's transformation into a commodity to be exploited (Tapper 2014, 85). In his book *One-Dimensional Man* (1964), Marcuse develops his theory of repressive desublimation which is "the systematic limitation on the scope of desublimation, the reduction of the sensual, pleasurable and erotic to specific sexual experiences ... leading to the general pursuit of false and limited wants and needs" (Held 1980, 108).

Such neo-Marxist ideas continue within the notes in the context of the eleventh Beck novel.

Concerning Ideology

The concept of ideology is important in Sjöwall-Wahlöö's work and the contexts in which it was composed. Therefore, I will briefly discuss the Marxist notion of ideology according to some thinkers who had a great influence in Sweden during the 1960s and 1970s: Besides Karl Marx, also Herbert Marcuse and Louis Althusser. These notions are some of the tools that we are going to use in the analysis of Sjöwall-Wahlöö since their novels often concern ideology and what ideology does to individuals in relation to crime and crime investigations.

According to Marx, "ideology is the system of ideas and representations which dominate the mind of a man or a social group". The French philosopher Louis Althusser also stresses that ideology for Marx is "an imaginary assemblage (*bricolage*), a pure dream" existing outside the history of individuals (Althusser 1970). This concept bears a complex relationship with Marxism, though. As we shall see there is another notion as presented by Marcuse. First, however, we might take a closer look at Althusser.

Althusser was introduced to Swedish readers as early as in 1966 through the journal *Clarté*, and later on the journal *Zenit* became the foremost Althusserian platform of the Swedish New Left (Ekelund 2014, 202–203). Zenit was also the first journal to introduce Marcuse to Swedish readers, in 1966 (Therborn 1966).

Althusser's conception of ideology does not include political ideologies as systems of thinking following Destutt de Tracy from the late eighteenth century, but more as world view, for example religious, political or philosophical views that make our world understandable. Marcuse's notion of ideology as false consciousness therefore is something other than Althusser's conception in which a philosophical term like truth is irrelevant (Ekelund 2014, 196).

The Althusserian concept of ideology is about how humans live their lives as conscious actors in a world that is more or less meaningful to them. He discards Marx's alienation theory as ideological (Žižek 2001, 9). Therborn describes this ideology as a medium where consciousness and meaningfulness is working, a mostly *unknown* process that shapes the human mind (Therborn 1981, 11). Althusser broke with the Marxist conception of ideology as a collection of ideas and thoughts when he saw it as a social process without a subject consisting of calls, or as he put it, "interpellations," to the human subjects (individuals) inside material social matrixes (Therborn 1981, 18). When every individual answers the interpellation they also confirm their own identity, via which every identity also has a given social coherence making it meaningful (Ekelund 2014, 222–23).

Althusser's "break" with the old Marxist tradition was a critique "from the left" against the Stalinist ideology of Soviet-Union during the 1950s, when Russian leader Nikita Khrushchev made a right turn in criticizing Stalin's murderous reign of terror. In this, Althusser also distanced himself from the Marxism as put forward by Marcuse and others, with the individual in the centre of ideology instead of structures and processes of power and economy (Nordin 2011, 547–48, Ekelund 2014, 197).

Althusser often came back to the motto of Lenin: without theory, there is no revolutionary practice. The philosophy of Althusser one could prescribe as a true participation in the struggle instead of sitting in an academic institution speculating with critical theory or the idealistic philosophy represented by philosophers like Horkheimer and Adorno (Ekelund 2014, 199–200).

To Althusser, ideology was something unbiased, created by the dialectical process, just like history. Individuals do not have anything to do with it. Or as Althusser put it: "An ideology always exists in an apparatus, and its practice, or practices. This existence is material" (Althusser 1970). Ideology is controlled by what he calls "Ideological State Apparatuses," for example the church, the state and its institutions. Each of them is the material realization of an ideology (Althusser 1970). Ideology appears through practices and rituals, not the reverse, according to Althusser. These rituals could be the mass in a church, a funeral, a soccer game, a day in school, or a political party meeting (Ekelund 2014, 222).

This view on ideology has been called anti-humanistic, meaning it does not put the individual but the structures at the core of the ideological process (Nordin 2011, 546). In fact, the individual is quite unimportant in this machinery; ideology is the very power that "interpellates" the individuals, and controls them, not the reverse.

The Frankfurt School, where Marcuse was one of the foremost philosophers from early 1930s, had been interested in the writings of the younger Marx which were discovered during the 1920s, in which the theory of alienation is central.

The human individual is the center of attention in the philosophy of Marcuse. He and the other critical theorists in the Frankfurt School developed, on the contrary to Lenin and Althusser, a non-Marxist thinking to *develop* Marxism with elements from Freud and Weber (Held 1980, 359–60). Althusser, on the other hand, thought that science could be demarcated from ideology, and not a result of it as Marcuse did (Held 1980, 359).

Marcuse continued along the line of the classic tradition from the Frankfurt School of the 1930s, in which German fascism was dissected, and during the 1960s he used the same critical methods on modern day capitalism in the United States where he had lived since the mid-1930s, and where he studied phenomena like bureaucracy, media manipulation and alienation.

To conclude: Althusser's focus on ideology is the structure; Marcuse's (and the Frankfurt School) is the individual as creator *and* victim of ideology. Human beings in society uphold ideology through economy, politics, art, culture, aesthetics, religion and so on. According to Althusser ideology is an objective process that interpellates the individuals in this society.

Source Material: The Last Words

Per Wahlöö's last words on paper, written sometime during the spring or summer of 1975, consist of two unlined sheets filled with hand-written text from top to bottom in different boxes. They include both short sentences and lengthier paragraphs. At the top of the first sheet there is an underlined title: "Gone to Earth," followed by the Swedish original: "Strax under ytan." The notes also list the co-authors as Maj Sjöwall and their son, Tetz, the setting, and a short publishing note, indicating that the book is not due for printing for a long time. According to Maj Sjöwall the book was to be written and then left in a safety deposit box for her and Wahlöö's children in the future. Sjöwall explained further that there are several ideas for other crime novels outlined on paper sheets deposited in the Swedish Royal Library in Stockholm (Sjöwall, personal interview August 28, 2013).

Per Wahlöö's last notes contain the outline of at least four new books, composing a series called The Ice Land Quartet, where the icy metaphor is obviously a representation of what Wahlöö and other communists thought of Sweden's chilling political state in the 1960s and '70s. His own experiences in hospitals become the focal point in these notes, and there are recurrent allusions to themes relating to death, aging, anxiety and the shortcomings of medical care. Looking at the notes, one can assume that "Gone to Earth" may have resembled a mixture of Swedish author P. C. Jersild's critique of hospitals in *House of Babel* (Babels hus, 1978), and Robin Cook's *Coma* (1977). The book was never written. All that remains is the outline of a narrative.

In the final years of his life, Wahlöö suffered from a number of complications arising from his condition; he died in Malmö Public Hospital in June 1975. One of Wahlöö's best friends at the time was journalist and writer Irka Cederberg. She is the prototype for Stalinist princess Rhea Nielsen who becomes romantically involved with Beck in the last three Beck novels. She and Wahlöö had talked about writing a novel together after the Martin Beck mysteries. It was going to be a crime story set in the underground tunnels of Malmö Public Hospital. During his final years Wahlöö often lived in different hospitals and became fascinated by the exciting underground area. But they never reached any kind of writing; just Wahlöö's own few words on paper (Cederberg, personal interview August 20, 2012).

According to Maj Sjöwall, there was never meant to be any more Martin Beck novels, she and Per had written ten of them already and that was it. Wahlöö was very weak when he wrote the last words and Sjöwall sees the notes as completely personal and private (Sjöwall, personal interview August 28, 2013).

Despite such assertions, those working in the crime fiction field will inevitably be interested in Wahlöö's plans. The main characters from the Beck series are all mentioned in the notes, ready to appear in the new narrative: Martin Beck, of course, as well as his police colleagues Lennart Kollberg, the abrasive Gunvald Larsson, rookie Benny Skacke, and Per Månsson. The story takes place in Malmö from winter to spring 1975; thus it neatly picks up the thread from the January 1975 setting of *The Terrorists*.

The notes for "Gone to Earth" indicate that the killer strikes his victims in the dark and deserted tunnels under the hospital. The reader learns that Berit, a nurse, takes a shortcut to work through an underground entrance to the hospital – an entrance usually blocked by locked doors between two main tunnels. In this obsolete and forgotten passage, she sees an abandoned bed and the corpse of what appears to be a murdered man. A doctor attributes the death to heart failure, but, following routine procedure, the dead man is taken to the pathologist. Here, Wahlöö hesitates about the cause of death, listing carelessness, a faulty organization, human error or negligence, and natural causes as possibilities. Eccentric Malmö police officer Per Månsson, who appears in several of the novels, gets the case. Månsson identifies it as murder and immediately calls for Beck and Skacke.

Theme 1: The Sexual Revolution
In the following I will discuss how sexuality in Sjöwall-Wahlöö's work relates to Wahlöö's last words. As noted in the introduction, I am also interested in

what ideology lies behind Wahlöö's female characters, and how these cone-cepts change over the course of the Sjöwall-Wahlöö legacy.

In the beginning of the 1960s sexual topics gained increasing importance in Swedish public debate. Controversial issues like sex education in schools, the deregulation of pornography and abortion, youngsters' – perhaps espe-cially young women' – right to their own sexuality, were discussed in news-papers, books, on radio, and on television around 1962, when Wahlöö was writing his books. In the mid-1960s this debate suddenly stopped when the Marxist turn gained a larger interest in issues such as the Vietnam War and class struggle (Lennerhed 1994, 9–10, 313, Östberg 2008, 341–42).

The main character in "Gone to Earth" is a 22-year-old nurse named Berit. Wahlöö sketches her as a young woman with extraordinary qualities, above all ethical, moral and professional ones. She is a wise and unaffected individ-ual convinced of the importance of Marxist thinking; like most of Wahlöö's female characters, she is average looking and disinterested in her appear-ance. The attentive reader can recall an older version of a nurse just like Berit in the 9th Beck novel *Cop Killer* (Polismördaren, 1974): "Because of vacancies, she was looking after two whole wards and had been at work for fourteen hours at a stretch, though she didn't show it. She was a serene, blond woman of about thirty-five, slim and strong, with clear eyes and muscular calves" (Sjö-wall-Wahlöö 1974, 198).

Beck's colleague Kollberg, who is a sensualist, looks at the ward nurse and muses: "How could she seem so fresh and healthy? With two wards to super-vise? She seemed cheerful enough. Clearly she must like her job" (Sjöwall-Wahlöö 1974, 198).

Almost the exact same thoughts figure in the notes for "Gone to Earth" when Wahlöö asks himself how she lives, how she can be so healthy. Does the North of Sweden offer better living? Wahlöö's conclusion about Berit is that she is a stable human individual who takes a firm stand against deprivation and decay. Clearly Wahlöö had an idealized image of nurses as fresh and healthy individuals, probably formed from his own extensive experience of hospitals.

The themes of sexuality and political awareness of Wahlöö are strongly linked together. In fact, there is a clear connection between sex-drive and political awareness in the Beck series that stretches back to the early nov-els of Per Wahlöö and continues in the portrait of Berit in "Gone to Earth." In Wahlöö's novels sexually liberated women become the representation of political (Marxist) awareness that initiate male characters into revolutionary thought. For example, Siglinde Pedersen in *A Necessary Action* (Lastbilen, 1962) (Hellgren 2015, 167). It is the story of Willy Mohr, an outcast German artist, drifter and former soldier, who has fled the destruction of post-war Germany to the paradise of the Spanish Balearic Islands. He becomes a part of the Bohemian atmosphere amongst Scandinavian artists in a small *puerto* during the 1950s, just before the dawn of mass tourism, but the fascist dictatorship is closing in on Mohr all the time. When a Norwegian couple, of which Siglinde Pedersen is the woman, gets murdered by two Spanish fishermen, Mohr turns into an avenger and the Spanish Guardia Civil pulls him in, interrogates him lengthily.

Siglinde Pedersen possesses "an immediate attractiveness, which appeared shallow and which made people think of sexuality ... in this phantom world of suppressed emotions" (Wahlöö 1962, 46). Her naked body stays in the mind of protagonist Willy Mohr and awakens his revolutionary thinking (Wahlöö 1962, 61).

The same kind of awakening comes to Manuel Ortega in *The Assignment* (Uppdraget, 1963) who initially is working as a foreign diplomat in Sweden and then goes back to his own country and sees the oppression of native citizens and a police state that is waging war against a communist rebel movement.

When Ortega meets mysterious secretary Danica Rodríguez, he suddenly starts to think about sex. "Why have I begun to think about these things so much?" he wonder (Wahlöö 1963, 83)? He starts thinking of her body. "When she walked away he stared at the thighs and hips. Earlier he had tried to decide whether she was wearing a bra but had been unable to come to any conclusion" (Wahlöö 1963, 86). Finally, Ortega has sex with her at the same time as she opens his eyes for the oppression of poor people in the country where they live.

It is likely that Danica Rodríguez is some kind of ideal woman in Wahlöö's gallery – politically conscious, sexually explicit – but as a bearer of ideological enlightenment and sexual awakening. Or even more clearly expressed; Danica could be seen as the embodied revolution, and Ortega, who is a highly regarded diplomat, is a part of the bourgeois ruling class, whose hegemony and ownership of the means of production in society gets exposed by Danica's Sexual-Marxism (Hellgren 2015, 192–94).

Another of Wahlöö's white-collar workers in a totalitarian state – just like Ortega – is Inspector Jensen, the prototype for Beck. In *Murder on the Thirty-first Floor* (Mord på 31:a våningen, 1964), he meets a sexually liberated woman opposing the repressive Orwellian society of the novel who reminds him of "women in pictures from the old days" (Wahlöö 1964, 146). In the sequel, *The Steel Spring* (1968), Jensen finally meets a nurse when he is at a hospital in the Soviet Union. This nurse resembles communist heroine Danica Rodríguez from *The Assignment* and *The Generals* (Generalerna, 1965). The nurse has the same effect on Jensen as Danica has on Ortega, and her characteristics are echoed later in Berit in "Gone to Earth": "She did not smoke or use any cosmetics, but she sometimes smelt of soap" (Wahlöö 1968, 23). He starts thinking about the nurse in sexual terms, a phenomenon, as in the case of Ortega, that is completely new to him; "he could not remember ever having thought anything like that before" (Wahlöö 1968, 23). This newly awakened sexual awareness breaks through what Marcuse refers to as the repressive des-ublimation associated with a totalitarian society and, upon his return to Swe-den, Jensen's thoughts turn to politics as he witnesses a full-scale communist revolution.

Yet, somewhere in the Beck series, this sexual motif changes. In *The Laugh-ing Policeman*, sexuality is associated with oppression rather than freedom and, at this point, sexuality becomes a commodity associated with the sex industries of prostitution and pornography. In this fourth instalment of Sjö-wall-Wahlöö, Beck and his colleagues investigate a mass murder on a bus. The man behind the massacre has also murdered a girl some 16 years earlier, and the crime has strong sexual implications.

In his analysis of *The Laughing Policeman* Tapper concludes that, concerning the initial spectacular mass murder on the bus, there is "a parallel between two death machines in the eyes of Sjöwall and Wahlöö – the United States and the Swedish welfare state" (Tapper 2014, 91). The killer is no longer a product of conformity that suddenly explodes in violence, like Folke Bengts-son in *Roseanna*, but instead the murderer Björn Forsberg in *The Laughing Policeman*, is an incarnation of capitalism which soon gets the full brunt of Sjöwall-Wahlöö's criticism. Tapper sees this novel as a "transition between the Freudian implications of the earlier novels and the Marxist subtext of the later ones" (Tapper 2014, 92).

What is interesting for us is the female victim Teresa Camarao, a Portuguese immigrant with an explicit sexual appetite. She is one of Wahlöö's many liter-ary nymphomaniacs, standing in the long line of Wahlöö's earlier sexually lib-erated women – and murder victims, Siglinde Pedersen in *A Necessary Action*, Roseanna McGraw in *Roseanna*, Danica Rodríguez in *The Assignment* and *The Generals*, Sigbrit Mård in *Cop Killer,* and in the final novel, *The Terrorists*, this kind of woman exists in Kristina Hellström (who does not get murdered, but commits suicide after being exploited by porn-producer Walter Petrus). An aspect that Tapper, Keetley (2012), and other scholars have overlooked is that these women are all the very opposite of what kills them: the male patriarchal hegemony of fascist Spain and Portugal, American capitalism and welfare state Sweden. The killers, in turn, represent the conformity of the welfare state, brutal fascism or American capitalism and greed.

Marcuse's repressive desublimation takes over; and, in the late novels of Sjö-wall-Wahlöö, pornography and capitalism become synonymous as rape and crimes against humanity. This change may be partly attributed to the Vietnam War, which exercised a profound influence on Swedish public debate in the mid-1960s, with the result that the New Left's interest in sexual issues became marginalized. In fact, the New Left often criticized early sex liberals for paving the way for the commercialization of sexuality (Lennerhed 1994, 313). Sjöwall-Wahlöö's most obvious response to this perception can be found in *The Terrorists* with its porn-film producer-villain.

According to Marxist theory, the individual is always under pressure from the socioeconomic conditions of society, conditions that will subdue the power of the working classes if they do not organize and take charge of the means of production (Eagleton 2011, 52, 148ff, Held 1980, 112). Wahlöö's nurses, in several of his novels – not just in the Beck series but also in his science-fiction thriller *The Steel Spring* – are often symbols of vibrant womanhood, freedom, and healthy sexuality. They become the perfect representation of the classic Marxist enlightened proletarian that consciously sees through the dark cloak of capitalist repressive desublimation, as outlined by Marcuse.

Dawn Keetley engages with this very important theme, positing that the image of the nymphomaniac embodies a "formlessness and disorder," not even fitting into the writers' carefully constructed social determinism in the Swedish class system: "Women's bodies thus constitute the blind spot of Sjö-wall and Wahlöö's trademark political critique" (Keetley 2012, 62). It is nonetheless possible to argue that the notion of sexuality in Sjöwall-Wahlöö's work is even more complicated than Keetley suggests.

As we have seen, sexuality as the symbol of freedom has a long tradition in the novels of Per Wahlöö, dating back to the early 1960s. Both Keetley and Tapper, contrary to many critics, have established that the early Beck novels are not, as previously thought, apolitical (Keetley 2012, 55). In his analysis of *Roseanna*, for example, Tapper reads the corpse of Roseanna McGraw, pulled from the muddy water, as a representation of pornography, violence against women, and sexual murders; in fact, as everything that has been hidden and denied within the Swedish Social-Democratic welfare state (Tapper 2014, 84–85). Tapper also talks about mass culture – imported American pulp cinema and violent comics – as the inspiration for Folke Bengtsson's crimes as they constitute the voice calling into his empty soul. Behind such artifacts of mass culture, there are perverse social structures making the killer a litmus paper for all the wars in the world, most notably the Vietnam War raging at the time. Bengtsson or, for that matter, Ingemund Fransson in *The Man on the Balcony* (1967), thus becomes the ultimate expression of a repressive and alienated normality (Tapper 2014, 86–87, 91).

Keetley, on the other hand, talks about *women's bodies* in crime fiction as "the inexplicable cause, of men's crimes, embodying the "natural" and uncontrollable impulses of both themselves and others" (Keetley 2012, 60). This is something an attentive reader may recognize from the novels of Raymond Chandler, perhaps most explicitly in *The Big Sleep* (1939), where sexually driven women set the plot in motion. It is, in fact, entirely probable that the figure of the nymphomaniac in Sjöwall-Wahlöö is taken from Chandler, who was a central influence on Wahlöö in the 1960s (Sjögren 1962).

Lena Lennerhed notes that the Swedish sexual liberalism of the 1960s represented a "stand for the freedom of the individual" (Lennerhed 1994, 312). The demands for free abortion, free access to pornography, less judgmental sex education in schools, and greater tolerance toward alternative sexualities was, she argues, important for the young generation during the first half of the 1960s (Lennerhed 1994, 307). Lennerhed concludes that Alfred Kinsey became a central character in the Swedish sexual debate when he asserted that "[m]en with an active sex life were … also more active on the whole" – a statement that challenged the psychoanalytic perspective of Freud who thought *sexual abstinence* would lead to greater intellectual activity (Lennerhed 1994, 308).

Marcuse, like Kinsey, stresses the connection between sexuality and freedom. In *Eros and Civilization* (1955), for example, Marcuse argues that sexuality can create highly civilized human relations; the goal of his new postrevolutionary society where lasting erotic relations between conscious, mature individuals is central. Sexuality would then be integrated with the order of work and play (Held 1980, 125). "The sex instincts are *life* instincts," says Marcuse in *Eros and Civilization* and further argues that the struggle for existence is a struggle for pleasure (Held 1980, 242).

Reading the novels of Wahlöö (and Sjöwall-Wahlöö) through the lens of

Marcuse thus explains the link between the often virile sexuality of Wahlöö's heroes and their leftist political radicalism. The sexual liberation theme, however, as previously mentioned, fades away in the latter novels and is replaced with a more Marxist critique of the commodification of sexuality.

Keetley talks about "men's perceived loss of power" as the root of the serial murders in the early Beck series (Keetley 2012, 56). That might well be the case, but sexuality as the negation of dictatorship and patriarchal fascism is the one clear thread working its way through every book Wahlöö has ever written. This thread – only slightly thinner – may also be seen in the final notes where nurse Berit is the clear representation of this sexually-free Marxist individual. Marcuse writes of the proletarian in the early stages of capitalism as "the living denial of his society" (Marcuse 1964, 28). Such sentiments accord with Wahlöö's views, not just of nurses and sexually liberated women, with Berit as his final example, but also with his misunderstood revolutionary killers, from Bertil Svensson to "Gone to Earth's" the Phantom.

Theme 2: The Oppressive Welfare State
In this chapter I will discuss Sjöwall-Wahlöö's notion of the oppressive welfare state. The main question will be how the notion of the oppressive welfare state in Sjöwall-Wahlöö correspond to the last words by Wahlöö, as well as which Marxist conception of ideology is presented by Sjöwall-Wahlöö and what impact the structure of the welfare state has on the individuals in the novels.

As early as 1965, in one of Sweden's most popular newspapers *Aftonbladet*, Sjöwall-Wahlöö presented their critique of the Swedish Social Democracy, just before they released their first co-written novel *Roseanna*. In their article the political bearing of Wahlöö's entire work comes to light. Sjöwall-Wahlöö's first words are: "You wake up every morning and wonder why the insurance system has not been socialized. You also wonder: Why monarchy?" (Sjöwall-Wahlöö 1965). Their critique of "the regime" refers of course to the Social Democratic government. Wahlöö had been disappointed with the Swedish labour movement ever since it had sold the weekly journal *Folket i Bild*, his old place of work, to capitalist media corporation Bonniers in 1962 (Hellgren 2015, 68). Further, Sjöwall-Wahlöö mention a "fearful socialism" based on cowardice and accord, and they also convey other political matters being given more attention at the time; increased child day care, a stop to the American military aggressions in the world, a public acknowledgement of East Germany, and military disarmament (Sjöwall-Wahlöö 1965).

It is also essential to understand the nature of the fictional world depicted by Sjöwall-Wahlöö during the mid-1970s. Dennis Lehane captures the mood of this world very nicely in his introduction to the American edition of *The Terrorists*:

> It's a late November world, compressed by a dark, swollen sky that hovers roughly four inches above your head until May. The courts don't work, the schools produce little but rot, and the ruling class skims the cream off the top and turns its back as the poor fight over the coffee grounds (Lehane 2013, x).

This world, as depicted by Lehane, is similar to what Marcuse outlines in *One-Dimensional Man*. The distinguishing feature of Marcuse's "advanced industrial society" is its effective suffocation of those needs that demand liberation (Marcuse 1964, 9). This society, furthermore, tends to be a totalitarian system "which operates through the manipulation of needs by vested interests" (Marcuse 1964, 5).

According to Wahlöö's notes, the setting and mood are roughly the same for "Gone to Earth." The proposed work, moreover, returns to the dystopian world depicted in Wahlöö's Marcusian crime/science fiction hybrid, *Murder on the Thirty-first Floor*; in this novel, a police state has taken control of society and, together with the capitalists, created a monstrous bureaucracy that resembles the one in George Orwell's *1984* (1949). Wahlöö's aim with his story is similar to the one that Maj Sjöwall describes for the Beck series: "under the official image of welfare-state Sweden there was another layer of poverty, criminality and brutality. We wanted to show where Sweden was heading: towards a capitalistic, cold and inhuman society, in which the rich got richer, the poor got poorer" (France 2009).

But the main critique in *Murder on the Thirty-First Floor* is that of capitalist monopoly press that exposes itself as the strangulation of freedom of speech, and in the long run results in capitalism as a democratic problem. Marcuse's thoughts are almost the same: "The products indoctrinate and manipulate; they promote a false consciousness which is immune against its falsehood" (Marcuse 1964, 14).

One-Dimensional Man was published in the same year as *Murder on the Thirty-First Floor*, and in his book Marcuse presents the notion of society as an economic-political rectification, just as Wahlöö does in his novel. This rectification, in turn, results inevitably in the manipulation of human needs. The words of Wahlöö in 1964 are strikingly similar to the philosophy of Marcuse:

> What they were attempting to do was to bring all the different points of view closer to each other. Perhaps it wasn't such a bad notion, but the methods that were being used to realise it were built almost entirely on hushing up any antagonism and difficulty. They lied away the problems. They glossed over them with constant improvements in material standards, and hid them behind a fog of meaningless talk pumped out via the radio, press and TV. And the phrase that covered it all was, then as now, "harmless entertainment." (Wahlöö 1964, 118)

Just as in sci-fi literature, Marcuse discusses the Utopian, and the importance of working out alternative conditions of society, and dialectical thinking, in this case, should then lead to an abstraction – an estrangement – of the empirical reality whose very existence then could be questioned. It is a world living in the shadow of the Cuban Missile Crisis and the emerging Vietnam War, whose very opposites in world politics is being constituted by the United States and the Soviet Union – a world threatened to be annihilated by the power game between these military super powers (Hellgren 2015, 278).

That is also exactly the same kind of state that is unveiled in both of Wahlöö's sci-fi novels – an existence where the foreboding threat of human extinction is central to thinking and philosophy. It is a world in which giant corporations have joined up with trade unions into lobbies and cartels, in which the natural opposition between labor and capital is being shrouded by "the Accord" made necessary by economical force – an existence in which the decrease of automation in the advanced industrial society leads to inevitable powerlessness and dispiritedness of the workers (Marcuse 1964, 40–41).

The central character in *Murder on the Thirty-First Floor* is the bleak Inspector Jensen, a traditional white-collar worker of the faceless dictatorship. Jensen gets to investigate a bomb threat against the tall newspaper building where all the media power is set. During his investigation he cruises through a world gone wrong that resembles a great deal of Chandler's "car society" in Los Angeles.

Wahlöö describes the Swedish capital Stockholm as a rough place (Wahlöö 1964, 88). The big crime is within the structure – what Althusser refers to as the ideological state apparatuses – the government, the corporations, the economy, the media, and the liberal ideology. Wahlöö eventually was trying to expose this particular crime for the rest of his life.

In his second novel about Inspector Jensen, *The Steel Spring*, released in 1968, the full blown image of this conspiracy is explained by a police doctor: "Capitalism's a crime in itself. But it's a paper tiger. If anyone drops a spanner in the works, it's got nothing to fall back on. People are indifferent to it. They know nothing and understand nothing beyond the narrow sector of their own training. And the alienation makes them incapable of establishing connections" (Wahlöö 1968, 199).

Of course, this is also the credo of Sjöwall-Wahlöö's Beck series; the exposure of the Social Democratic government as a bourgeois "Accord", a corporate state, in close cooperation with big corporations at the expense of the working class and Socialism.

Ideologically, Wahlöö's idea of history also joins the Marxist narrative of a chronological transition from capitalism to socialism, and the story of contemporary time as a crisis of capitalism, what Lenin thought of as a *revolutionary situation* (Lenin 1913).

In *The Terrorists*, the lawyer Hedobald Braxén, also known as Crasher, is allowed to speak for the authors when he declares:

> For as long as I can remember, large and powerful nations within the capitalist bloc have been ruled by people who according to accepted legal norms are simply criminals, who from a lust for power and financial gain have led their peoples into an abyss of egoism, self-indulgence and a view of life based entirely on materialism and ruthlessness toward their fellow human beings. ... Someone once said that our country is a small but hungry capitalist state. This judgment is correct. For a pure-hearted thinking person ... a system such as ours must seem incomprehensible and hostile. She realized however, that someone must bear the responsibility, and when this person cannot be reached or contacted by ordinary human methods, she is overwhelmed with despair and mindless hatred. (Sjöwall-Wahlöö 1975, 231)

This ideological view – in which the individual is essential – of the welfare state Wahlöö had developed through his entire corpus, and his last notes follow this with the outline of a murder plot in which the pure-hearted (leftist) individual is the victim of a criminal regime.

The politicization and proletarianization of crime novels that Sjöwall-
Wahlöö initiated with the Beck series was, it is clear, set to continue with
"Gone to Earth." The notes also show that Wahlöö had clear plans to weave
his views on Swedish medical care into the novel. For example, they include
a notation of how a truck driver can, according to law, only work for approxi-
mately seven hours, whereas an emergency, on-call surgeon is expected to
cope with 36- to 48-hour stretches over a weekend. Similarly, a ward nurse
works from early morning to late evening and carries the responsibility for
50 to 100 patients. Wahlöö is clear in his view on this problem: The fault
lies with the politicians and bureaucracy. Hence, the system and its fail-
ings become the motive for the crimes committed in several of the Sjöwall-
Wahlöö novels.

The main character in "Gone to Earth," Berit, seems to be a young and genuine human – a sociological indicator of the flattened Swedish welfare state, all
boiled down into one person, her actions, and her morals. She is a product of
the New Leninist left and represents what Östberg portrays as "a re-affiliation
to an older tradition within the Marxist movement, dating to a period when
the industrial proletarian was the revolution's bearer" (Östberg 2008, 349).
The same type of character reappears in several of Sjöwall-Wahlöö's novels,
all of them in some way victims of the ideological state apparatuses – the
institutions of the welfare state. For example, the poor young hippie Rebecka
Lind is turned into a robber and political assassin in *The Terrorists*, whereas
tough-girl Monita, in *The Locked Room* (Det slutna rummet, 1972), is forced
by circumstances (according to Marxist sociology) to be a thief: "For a while
Monita had been out of work. She recieved a meager income from unemploy-
ment insurance but became steadily more depressed. All her thoughts went to
the problem of how to make ends meet; rent, food, and clothes for Mona swal-
lowed up everything she could scrape together" (Sjöwall-Wahlöö 1972, 195).
Yet another example could be found in *Cop Killer*, in which young small-time
crook Kasper gets falsely accused of having killed a police officer and then
chased all over Sweden. It is the now well-worn recipe for Sjöwall-Wahlöö's
narrative arc: the criminal as victim of bourgeois capitalist society and its
socio-economic doctrines (see, for example, Brodén 2011, 103).

In "Gone to Earth," Wahlöö describes the killer as some kind of qualified
blue-collar worker, perhaps a licensed welder, who has been harassed by the
bureaucracy until he breaks – the Union, the Bureau of Child Welfare, the
Social Insurance Office – Althusser's ideological state apparatuses all over
again. A long ensuing stay at the hospital provides him with a good under-

standing of the environment and those within it. Readers familiar with the Beck series will recognize this type of criminal – the criminal as victim – from *The Abominable Man* (Den vedervärdige mannen från Säffle, 1971) in which frustrated avenging ex-cop Åke Eriksson climbs the rooftops of Stockholm and starts targeting police officers with a rifle when he finds out that his wife, sick with diabetes, has died in police custody.

In *The Terrorists*, this kind of character appears as the gardener Sture Hellström, who takes his revenge on porn film-producer Walter Petrus, responsible for the death of Hellström's daughter. A third example – perhaps the most explicit one – may be found in the working-class vigilante Bertil Svensson in *Murder at the Savoy* (1970), who executes the villainous CEO, Viktor Palmgren, at an upper-class dining table in the midst of a business dinner at the Malmö Hotel Savoy. Here, the killer becomes an avenger against the capitalistic welfare state and its ideological state apparatuses: the very foundations for the oppression of humanity in both the Althusserian and Marcusian sense. The killer strikes back on the bureaucratic conglomerate created by the Swedish Social Democratic government and capitalism; a creation known as the Swedish Model, which results in the very same type of deserted society as that of Marcuse's *One-Dimensional Man*: a society dominated by the "unification of opposites" which becomes a blocking for social change (Marcuse 1964, 22).

Returning to *Murder at the Savoy*, J. Kenneth Van Dover identifies the "revolutionary awareness" inherent in Svensson's shooting of Palmgren: "Just as Palmgren is an unqualified emblem of greedy, destructive capitalism, so the killer represents the oppressed proletariat rising in sudden, revolutionary awareness of the source of its ills" (Van Dover 1993, 45). The killer belongs to what Marcuse refers to as

> …the substratum of the outcasts and outsiders, the exploited and persecuted of other races and other colors, the unemployed and the unemployable. They exist outside the democratic process; their life is the most immediate and the most real need for ending intolerable conditions and institutions. Thus their opposition is revolutionary even if their consciousness is not. (Marcuse 1964, 260)

The chilling Swedish welfare state thus provides fertile ground for the entire Beck series, and "Gone to Earth" fits very nicely into this pattern. As Sean and Nicci French suggest in their introduction to *The Laughing Policeman*, the novel is characterized by "a sense that something has gone profoundly wrong in Social Democratic Sweden, as if the crimes he [Beck] faces are superficial symptoms of a much deeper historical crisis" (French 2011, vii). This connects to the social theory of Marcuse, as he talks of this society as a historical project gone wrong: "an omnipresent system which swallows up or repulses all alternatives" (Marcuse 1964, xlvii).

Still, this notion of the welfare state was not unique to Marxist or left-wing writers during the 1960s and '70s. Swedish intellectual historian David Östlund (2007) made a steep dive straight into conservative Roland Huntford's book *The New Totalitarians* (1971), with its harsh critique of the Swedish welfare state, also known as the People's Home (*Folkhemmet*). Despite Huntford's right-wing position, his argument aligns closely with those of left-wing writers like Wahlöö and their criticism of the Swedish People's Home. According to Huntford, a totalitarian state was hiding behind the Swedish veil of false democracy. He writes of the Swedes as a pure collectivist people, an uncritical mass forever duped by "the rulers" of a totalitarian regime that was connected to a Russian world of Eastern dystopia (Östlund 2007, 50). Östlund also puts Huntford's dystopia into a broader literary context, adopting Aldous Huxley's *Brave New World* (1932) and Orwell's *1984* as marks of historical reference (Östlund 2007, 51).

Tapper repeatedly connects Huntford's image of Sweden with the crime novels of Sjöwall-Wahlöö (Tapper 2014, 67, 77, 87). Like Östlund, he also aligns this to the German Frankfurt School, particularly Marcuse, whose notions of an instrumental reason that manipulates people fits like a glove with the image of Sweden portrayed by Huntford and Sjöwall-Wahlöö. Just like the Swedish left in the 1960s, Huntford also saw a class-traitorous conspiracy behind the Swedish model of understanding and its world-famous method for class collaboration (Östlund 2007, 60).

Wahlöö returns to the notion of the criminal as victim in this society in "Gone to Earth" when he draws up the final sequence, sketching it as violent and action-oriented in the style of *The Abominable Man*. The killer is obviously driven by the media and his own planning into an absurd situation he cannot control. In the end, he identifies himself with the construction of himself presented by the media, which calls him "the Phantom of the tunnel." Media, in this case, could be seen as another one of Althusser's ideological state apparatuses that "interpellates" the Phantom, who confirms his projected identity and becomes something that he is probably not. The notes make reference to wild chases and an atmosphere of terror, indicating that Beck steps in and solves the case by searching through the past lives of the murder victims.

Daniel Brodén argues that the Swedish People's Home provides a central point of reference to modern police films and, moreover, that the downfall of the welfare state in Sjöwall-Wahlöö has set the tone for subsequent crime films and novels. Another important historical reference in this case is the forming of a central Swedish police authority called *Rikspolisstyrelsen* in 1964 and the rhetoric surrounding an ideal of the white-collar worker in society (Brodén 2008, 191). Therefore, there are clear links among an escalating social criticism, the growth of crime fiction, and a growing modern bureaucracy: A capitalist society that, according to Sjöwall-Wahlöö, permits "a criminal exploitation of its citizens" (Brodén 2008, 196). In line with Sjöwall-Wahlöö's complete corpus, Wahlöö in his notes finally settles the killer's credo: He is pursuing a derailed crusade against the same bureacracy that is breaking him down.

Conclusion

This article has been divided into two different themes – the sexual revolution and the oppression of the welfare state – investigated with a starting point in the recently discovered last notes of Per Wahlöö written in 1975. The two themes are important, and perhaps the main themes in the entire Sjöwall-Wahlöö legacy. Especially the latter theme has been used by more contemporary writers in the genre, such as Henning Mankell and Stieg Larsson, whose stories explore the dark world of Sweden during the 1990s and 2000s.

My first main question was how sexuality in Sjöwall-Wahlöö corresponds to the last words by Wahlöö?

The sexual matters have been toned down in the last words but the themes of class-struggle and the oppressed criminal as a victim are still there, also dominating the Swedish public debate at the time. But the main character, nurse Berit, is one of those sexually liberated women Wahlöö has always written about, Marxist thinking and politically aware, the very opposite of fascism, capitalism and the tormenting Swedish bureaucracy. She is the final image of the Sexual-Marxist woman that has followed Wahlöö ever since the early '60s.

An underlying question has also been what ideology lay behind Wahlöö's female characters?

This ideology could be called Sexual-Marxism, in this case meaning the ideology and theories developed by thinkers like Herbert Marcuse and Wilhelm Reich: individual and revolutionary emancipation through sexual communication. Althusser's concept "interpellation" could be used in this sense as well; when the female characters "interpellate" the male counterparts, stirring their thoughts to become politically conscious – or, as we also have seen, murderous maniacs. This theory on sexual emancipation is perhaps my most important contribution in this article, and it signals a break with scholars like Keetley and Tapper who have different analyses of the sexual issues of Sjöwall-Wahlöö.

Another underlying question in the sexual theme was how the conception of women change through the Sjöwall-Wahlöö legacy?

A careful reading indicates that it goes through a radical transformation over the years; from being revolutionary subjects, imposing critical thought into the male protagonists up till the mid-1960s, to become exploited by capitalists and the sex industry in the 1970s. In 1968 the sexual revolution suddenly turned into slavery when Teresa Camarao was first prostituted and then murdered in *The Laughing Policeman*. After that the women of Sjöwall-Wahlöö became strangled, shot and committed suicide, but soon they also started to fight back, and eventually Wahlöö created the character Rhea Nielsen, a strong communist heroine that became the mistress of Beck in the final three novels of the series. At that point Beck meets the same destiny as Ortega, Mohr and Jensen in Wahlöö's earlier novels; he turns into a politically conscious, and sexually liberated, human being after the long and suffocating marriage with Inga Beck in the first half of the series (Bergman 2014, 41, Tapper 2014, 97). By that time – in 1975 – sexual issues had been widely brushed aside by class matters, just as they were in public debate during the 1970s.

In the analysis of my second theme, regarding the oppressive welfare state, the main question was how this notion responds to the last words of Wahlöö, and an underlying question is what impact the structures of the welfare state have on the individuals in the novels?

First of all, it is the very same dark November world in "Gone to Earth" that appears in novels like *Cop Killer* and *The Terrorists*. Ideological state apparatuses like the Social Insurance Office and the Bureau of Child Welfare have been harassing the killer – "the Phantom" – in the story. But unlike other criminals in the Beck series he identifies with the call – the "interpellation" – coming from the system, in this case the media. He suddenly becomes a conscious "actor" within the ideological, social process that Althusser is talking about. Although the Phantom rises in sudden revolutionary action he is not necessarily a revolutionary individual. He might just be a human being with a false consciousness – just like everybody else, according to the Marcusian theory of repressive desublimation.

This takes us into the discussion of which ideology is represented by Sjö-wall-Wahlöö.

The human individual is always central in the entire Sjöwall-Wahlöö series, from the early 1960s to the very end. The structures and social processes that Althusser stresses in his conception of ideology dominate the later novels, although alienation and other aspects of Marcusian theories are predomi-nant in the early novels. At the same time Sjöwall-Wahlöö's notion of the wel-fare state in the later novels resemble to right-wing ideas from a conservative writer like Roland Huntford.

The revolutionary theory dominates the latter novels with killers like Bertil Svensson and Åke Eriksson, and both Althusser and Marcuse are revolution-ary theorists, although their revolutionary subjects are different from each other. Althusser has adopted Lenin's notion of the party elite taking charge of the process, leading the masses into communism. Marcuse mentions the outcasts, the unemployed, and the oppressed people in the colonies as those who need a revolution the most (Held 1980, 76). This idea is probably the one that is most similar to the political agenda in Sjöwall-Wahlöö's writings.

Finally, it might be concluded that Wahlöö should be unhappy with the Phantom's revenge on society in "Gone to Earth," since he does not seem to be ideologically conscious. I would say that he is manipulated rather than conscious. However, that is also the never-ending problem in all of Wahlöö's writings, from the early novels of the 1960s, in which Spanish repression causes the same outbursts of violence, to the Beck series, in which individual criminals appear as victims of a class struggle they don't seem to understand. Marcuse's notion of the criminal as victim is captured in the statement that "according to Freud, the patient's disease is a protest reaction against the sick world in which he lives" (Marcuse 1964, 188). He also talks of this kind of person, the outcast, as the true revolutionary in society, "an elementary force which violates the rules of the game and, in doing so, reveals it as a rigged game" (Marcuse 1964, 261).

All of Wahlöö's characters during a period of fifteen years could thus be seen as victims of this rigged game, from his first Spanish novel, *The Wind and the Rain* (1961), to his last words in the book that went up in smoke, "Gone to Earth."

References

Althusser, Louis. 1970. "Ideology and Ideological State Apparatuses (Notes towards an Investigation)". Accessed June 29, 2015. https://www.marxists.org/reference/archive/althusser/1970/ideology.htm.

Bergman, Kerstin. 2014. *Swedish Crime Fiction: The Making of Nordic Noir.* Mimesis International.

Brodén, Daniel. 2008. *Folkhemmets skuggbilder: En kulturanalytisk genrestudie av svensk kriminalfiktion i film och tv* [Dark Shadows of the Welfare State: A Cultural Genre History of Crime Fiction in Swedish Cinema and Television]. Stockholm: Ekholm & Tegebjer.

———. 2011. "The Dark Ambivalences of the Welfare State: Investigating the Transformations of the Swedish Crime Film." In *Northern Lights* 9: 95–109.

Eagleton, Terry. 2011. *Varför Marx hade rätt* [Why Marx Was Right]. Translated by Maria Åsard. Stockholm: Tankekraft.

Ekelund, Alexander. 2014. "Kampen om vetenskapen. Althusserianismens frammarsch och den svenska 1968-vänsterns vetenskapsteoretiska debatt." [The Struggle on Science: The Advance of Althusserianism and the Scientific Theoretical Debate of the Swedish 1968-Left]. In *Tillsammans. Politik, filosofi och estetik på 1960- och 1970-talen* [Together: Politics, Philosophy and Aesthetics in the 1960s and '70s], ed. Anders Burman and Lena Lennerhed, 191–229. Stockholm: Atlas.

France, Louise. 2009. "The Queen of Crime." *The Observer,* November 22. Accessed February 27, 2015. http://www.theguardian.com/books/2009/nov/22/crime-thriller-maj-sjowall-sweden.

French, Sean, and Nicci. 2011. Introduction to *The Laughing Policeman* by Sjöwall-Wahlöö, v–viii. London: Fourth Estate.

Hellgren, Per. 2015. *Nu rasar diktaturerna. Per Wahlöö och vägen till den nya kriminalromanen* [Per Wahlöö. Paving the Way for Swedish Crime Fiction]. Malmö: Universus Academic Press.

Held, David. 1980. *Introduction to Critical Theory: Horkheimer to Habermas.* Oxford: Polity Press, 2004.

Holmberg, John-Henri. 2014. *A Darker Shade of Sweden.* New York: The Mysterious Press.

Jenkins, David. 1968. *Sweden and the Price of Progress.* New York: Coward.

Jersild, P. C. 1978. *House of Babel.* Lincoln: University of Nebraska Press.

Keetley, Dawn. 2012. "Unruly Bodies: The Politics of Sex in Maj Sjöwall and Per Wahlöö's Martin Beck Series." *Clues. A Journal of Detection* 1: 54–64.

Lehane, Dennis. 2013. Introduction to *The Terrorists* by Sjöwall-Wahlöö, ix–xii. New York: Vintage Books.

Lenin, V. I. 1913. "May Day Action by the Revolutionary Proletariat." Accessed July 27, 2015. https://www.marxists.org/archive/lenin/works/1913/jun/15.htm.

Lennerhed, Lena. 1994. *Frihet att njuta. Sexualdebatten i Sverige på 1960-talet* [The Pursuit of Pleasure. The Sex-Debate in Sweden during the 1960s]. Stockholm: Norstedts.

Mankell, Henning. 2012. Preface to *Roseanna* by Sjöwall-Wahlöö, 5–9. Stockholm: Piratförlaget.

Marcuse, Herbert. 1964. *One-Dimensional Man*. London: Routledge, 2002.

Nordin, Svante. 2011. *Filosoferna. Det västerländska tänkandet sedan år 1900* [The Philosophers: Western Thinking Since Year 1900]. Stockholm: Atlantis.

Östberg, Kjell. 2008. "Sweden and the Long '1968': Break or Continuity?" *Scandinavian Journal of History* 33: 339–52.

Östlund, David. 2007. "Maskinmodernitet och dystopisk lycka: den sociala ingenjörskonstens Sverige, upplaga Huntford 1971" [Machine Modernity and Dystopical Happiness: The Social Engineering of Sweden, Huntford Edition 1971.] *Polhem: Teknikhistorisk årsbok*: 40–63.

Reich, Wilhelm. 1933. *The Mass Psychology of Fascism* [Die Massenpsychologie des Faschismus]. 3rd ed. Translated by Mary Boyd Higgins. New York: Farrar, Straus and Giroux, 1980.

Sjögren, Henrik. 1962. "Studier i diktatur" [Studies in Dictatorship]. *Kvällsposten*, June 30.

Sjöwall, Maj, and Per Wahlöö. 1965. *Roseanna*, Stockholm: Piratförlaget, 2012.

———. 1965. "Vi är alla tillfredsställda – men på låtsas" [We Are All Satisfied – But Just Pretending]. *Aftonbladet*, August 26.

———. 1968. *The Laughing Policeman*. Translated by Alan Blair. London: Fourth Estate, 2011.

———. 1972. *The Locked Room*. Translated by Paul Britten Austin. London: Victor Gollancz Ltd., 1974.

———. 1974. *Cop Killer*. Translated by Thomas Teal. London: Victor Gollancz Ltd., 1975.

———. 1975. *The Terrorists*. Translated by Joan Tate. New York: Vintage Books, 2013.

Tapper, Michael. 2014. *Swedish Cops. From Sjöwall & Wahlöö to Stieg Larsson*. Bristol: Intellect.

Therborn, Göran. 1966. "Samhället som aktiebolag – Mot ett endimensionellt samhälle" [Society as Corporation – Towards a One-Dimensional Society]. *Zenit* 2–3: 4–7.

———. 1981. *Maktens ideologi och ideologins makt* [The Ideology of Power and the Power of Ideology]. Lund: Zenit.

Van Dover, J. Kenneth. 1993. *Polemical Pulps: The Martin Beck Novels of Maj Sjö-wall and Per Wahlöö*. San Bernadino, CA: Brownstone Books.

Wahlöö, Per. 1962. *A Necessary Action*. Translated by Joan Tate. New York: Vintage Books, 2013.

———. 1963. *The Assignment*. Translated by Joan Tate. New York: Vintage Books, 2013.

———. 1964. *Murder on the Thirty-first Floor*. Translated by Sarah Death. New York: Vintage Books, 2013.

———. 1968. *The Steel Spring*. Translated by Sarah Death. London: Vintage Books, 2011.

Wendelius, Lars. 1999. *Rationalitet och kaos. Nedslag i svensk kriminalfiktion efter 1965* [Rationality and Chaos. Case Studies in Swedish Crime Fiction after 1965]. Hedemora: Gidlunds.

Zizek, Slavoj. 2001. *Ideologins sublima objekt* [The Sublime Object of Ideology]. Translated by Lars Nylander. Göteborg: Glänta.

Unpublished material:

Wahlöö, Per. 1975. "Gone to Earth"/"Strax under ytan." [Two sheets of paper]. Photocopy in the possession of Irka Cederberg, Malmö, Sweden.

Interviews:

Cederberg, Irka. Personal Interview. Aug. 20, 2012.

Cederberg, Irka. Personal Interview. Feb. 29, 2012.

Sjöwall, Maj. Personal Interview. Aug. 20, 2012.

Sjöwall, Maj. Personal Interview. Aug. 28, 2013.

www.ingramcontent.com/pod-product-compliance
Lightning Source LLC
Chambersburg PA
CBHW020400130626
46549CB00006B/2370